Jennifer Stone worked as a journalist in London for several years. She has now moved to the Geneva border of France to join her husband who is at the United Nations. They have a small daughter.

'There will be no stopping the curious cook when this boozy book comes into the kitchen because it fires the imagination and gets the taste buds working'
Country Life

Jennifer Stone

The
Alcoholic Cookbook

Illustrations by Kate Simunek

MAYFLOWER
GRANADA PUBLISHING
London Toronto Sydney New York

Published by Granada Publishing Limited
in Mayflower Books 1978

ISBN 0 583 12528 X

First published in Great Britain by
Michael Joseph Ltd 1972
Copyright © Jennifer Stone 1972

Granada Publishing Limited
Frogmore, St Albans, Herts AL2 2NF
and
3 Upper James Street, London W1R 4BP
1221 Avenue of the Americas, New York, NY 10020, USA
117 York Street, Sydney, NSW 2000, Australia
100 Skyway Avenue, Toronto, Ontario, Canada M9W 3A6
Trio City, Coventry Street, Johannesburg 2001, South Africa
CML Centre, Queen & Wyndham, Auckland 1, New Zealand

Made and printed in Great Britain by
Richard Clay (The Chaucer Press) Ltd
Bungay, Suffolk
Set in Linotype Times

For
Peter with love

CONTENTS

ACKNOWLEDGEMENTS

Anybody who cooks does so for two reasons: to survive, or ensure the survival of others, and to delight.

Those of us who cook to delight learn our skills everywhere and I am grateful to my teachers. Starting with my mother who encouraged me to cook almost as soon as she encouraged me to read, and then to all the people who have written cookery books and articles that have amused, inspired, outraged and titillated me.

In the first year of being married my bedtime reading was always a cookery book, much to the amusement of my husband who couldn't understand the pleasure to be had from reading about food as opposed to eating it.

And I am grateful to my husband who ate everything I made, helped me and bullied me away from the ambitious three-course dinners that were never ready until midnight. I'm only sorry his waistline suffered.

I'm also very grateful to all my friends who swapped boozy recipes, and who helped me reject all complicated and pretentious recipes. Everything in this book is as uncomplicated as possible.

Without Jane Hoyle's help this book would have been finished, but heaven knows when.

Thank you all.

INTRODUCTION

Why eat it when you can drink it? Why should anyone pour good alcohol into a cooking pot?

Because it's the simplest way of turning yourself into the sort of cook that is the envy of all the people lucky enough to be invited by her to dinner.

Because it's the quickest way of producing a superlative meal.

And because, believe it or not, it is frequently the *cheapest* way of producing something out-of-the-ordinary.

And there are beneficial side effects as well. If you're cooking with a bottle of sherry, wine, beer or whatever at your elbow, you might as well take a drink at the same time as you add a little to your recipe. Hence it is being used to improve your masterpiece, and your temper. Happiness all round. And the happy cook is the good cook.

So if you're like me, this method is for you. Much as I love cooking, dearly as I love my friends, I do also have a house to run, to say nothing of a full-time job. So if ever I am to see a film, read a book, climb a mountain or write a letter, my cooking has to be speedy. It has to fit in with other things.

Alcohol is the key to all this. Even in the simplest dishes. Even with something as British as that classic stand-by, roast beef.

What do I do with roast beef, for goodness' sake? Well, I do something to the gravy.

It should never taste like that thick lumpy stuff made from flour and meat cubes. Throw away all the packets food manufacturers try to convince you are essential for producing good gravy.

In the roasting pan stir a good tablespoonful of flour into

a sizeable quantity of fat from the meat. Stir really well and scrape up all the bits. When everything is absorbed add some wine and stirring diligently bring the gravy to a boil, if it is thick add more wine, or vegetable water, or stock if you have any. Just before serving stir in a good dollop of cream. Quantities depend on how many you're feeding and whether you like thin gravy.

Don't worry too much about the cost. While it is obviously hopelessly extravagant to make a trip to the off-licence to buy a bottle of whisky to pour on your tinned peaches, it is hardly wanton profligacy to help yourself to the equivalent of a small nip from a bottle of whatever you happen to have in the drinks cupboard. It's quite likely your man does anyway. Just as you don't use a whole packet of flour at a time, neither do you pour a whole bottle of fine burgundy into a casserole with a chicken for *coq au vin*.

Never use good wines for cooking. Never. Ever. Or not unless money really is as nothing to you.

Despite what many experts will tell you – in their friendly arrogance – it is not necessary to cook with the wines you plan to drink. Nor is it essential to use top-class sherry for syllabub, or fine champagne cognac for brandy butter. Sheer madness in my opinion.

So low has the quality of the wine I use for cooking sunk, that I once made a beef and wine stew with nine-tenths of a bottle of red plonk opened two days before that had turned vinegary. The result was quite delicious and we certainly didn't feel we should have drunk vinegar with it.

The whole question of cost gets so distorted it is almost impossible to argue rationally. Some people, who spend what I consider a small fortune on fillet steak and lobster, reckon that I waste money when I pour white wine on cod. And while many a man will not allow his wife to use a glass of brandy for cooking he will happily take her out to a £10 dinner and have brandy with coffee as well.

But if you are not completely broke, do want to produce above-average food, but do not have half a day to prepare your better meals: try cooking my way, with alcohol … hic!

Starters

Avocados with Grapes

This is a different way of tarting up one of the old faithfuls.

3 ripe avocado pears
lemon juice
675 g (1 lb 8 oz) muscatel grapes
6 tablespoons Madeira or sweet sherry.

Prepare the avocados as usual. Brush the insides freely with lemon juice to prevent discolouring. Chill. Halve the grapes and remove the pips. Fill the pear halves with the grapes and sprinkle with the wine.

SERVES 6.

Avocado Mousse

I first had this at a restaurant and then searched just about every cookbook ever written to find out how to make it. A journalist friend finally told me – it's so easy, anyone can manage it.

3 very ripe avocados
1 carton sour cream
3 tablespoons sweet sherry
salt and freshly ground black pepper

Skin and stone the avocados. Using a silver fork mash them until smooth. Some people liquidize them but this I don't care for: firstly the consistency is too smooth and secondly you waste an awful lot of avocado which is sinful at the price they are. Then stir in the cream, sherry and seasoning. Store in the fridge until needed or serve at once. If this is to be stored it must be kept in a bowl in a polythene bag or in Tupperware, if the air is not kept out the lovely pale green colour goes and you are left with an unattractive donkey brown. It's delicious, though as avocados have a slightly liverish reputation I wouldn't serve this before, say, a mousse.

SERVES 6 (or more if the avocados are large).

Artichoke Mousse

This vegetable has never been very popular, but I think it has an interesting taste.

900 g (2 lb) Jerusalem artichokes
2½ teaspoons gelatine
½ cup water
¾ glass sherry
4 eggs
150 ml (¼ pint) double cream

Peel the artichokes and boil in salted water for about 15 minutes. Drain, mash and sieve.

Mix the gelatine and water together and put on a low heat until the gelatine has dissolved. Add to the purée together with the sherry and leave to cool a little.

Separate the eggs. Lightly whisk the yolks and add to the purée. Season well and leave in a cool place until just beginning to set.

Beat the egg whites until very stiff, and also beat the cream. As the purée begins to set, fold them both in. Pour into individual ramekins or a soufflé dish.

SERVES 6 to 8.

Italian Aubergines

Can be served as a first course or as a supper dish either hot or cold.

3 aubergines
salt
cooking oil
1 tablespoon butter
1 tablespoon flour
about 150 ml (¼ pint) milk
50 g (2 oz) grated cheese
125g (4 oz) peeled and sliced button mushrooms
125 g (4 oz) ham, chopped

2 tablespoons white wine *or* sherry
1 tablespoon cream
seasoning

Cut the aubergines in half lengthwise. With a knife cut
round the edge of the inside about 2½ cm (1 inch) deep and
make several insertions across the flesh in the middle.
Sprinkle them with salt and leave to stand for about 1
hour. Pour off the liquid and wipe off the salt. Heat some
cooking oil and fry, turning once or twice, for about 10
minutes. Drain on absorbent paper.

Melt the butter and flour and stir in enough milk to make
a thick white sauce. Add the cheese, reserving some to
sprinkle on top of the aubergines before cooking them, and
stir until dissolved. Add the mushrooms, ham, white wine
or sherry, cream and season well.

Scoop out the middle of the aubergines, being careful
not to damage the skin. Dice it and add to the sauce. Fill
the aubergine skins with the mixture and sprinkle the
grated cheese on top. Bake in a hot oven for about 7 to 10
minutes.

SERVES 6.

Gloucestershire Rarebit

An excellent supper dish, or served more delicately as here
gives pleasure as a first course. Cheap and filling.

225 g (8 oz) Double Gloucester cheese (or any strong
    hard cheese)
mustard
275 ml (½ pint) ale
thick slices bread
butter

Flake or coarsely grate the cheese into a fireproof dish.
Spread mustard to taste over the cheese and pour in the
ale. Bake in a low oven until the cheese is dissolved. Toast
the bread, butter it and sprinkle the buttered side with a

little extra ale. Pour the sauce over and serve at once.

SERVES 4.

Baked Eggs with Pâté

Effortless, delicious and just the thing to use up spare pâté.

> Butter
> 4 6 mm (¼ in) slices fine pâté, i.e. chicken liver, foie gras, kipper *or* sardine
> salt and plenty of pepper
> 4 dessertspoons liquor to match pâté, i.e. brandy with chicken liver, Madeira with foie gras, white wine with kipper
> 4 or 8 eggs

Butter your ramekins extremely generously (otherwise the washing up will be hell). Place a round of pâté in the bottom of each. Be liberal with the salt and pepper. Pour on the liquor. Gently break in one or two eggs to taste (i.e. depending on how substantial the rest of the meal is to be). Stand in a roasting dish of hot water and bake in a moderate oven for 15 minutes.

SERVES 4.

Baked Eggs with Mustard, Cheese and Wine

This is exceptionally good.

> 50 g (2 oz) grated Gruyère cheese
> 2 teaspoons prepared Swiss *or* French mustard
> 2 tablespoons dry white wine
> salt
> 2 cartons sour cream
> 12 eggs
> buttered breadcrumbs

Mix the cheese, mustard, wine and salt with the cream.

Grease with buttered paper six individual ramekins. Break two eggs into each and top with the sauce and sprinkle with breadcrumbs. Stand the ramekins in a roasting tin half filled with water and bake in a moderate oven for 15 minutes.

SERVES 6.

If you use less cream the cheese mixture can be used to make an excellent supper dish. Toast bread on one side, turn it over, spread with the mixture and grill until it bubbles. Delicious.

Eggs baked in a Mushroom Sauce

More unusual than eggs baked in cream and a pleasant change.

> 225 g (8 oz) button mushrooms
> 75 g (3 oz) butter
> 2 tablespoons flour
> 275 ml ($\frac{1}{2}$ pint) chicken stock } *or* 550 ml (1 pint)
> 275 ml ($\frac{1}{2}$ pint) chicken stock } dry white wine
> 3 tablespoons good mayonnaise
> 1 chopped chive
> several sprigs chopped parsley
> salt and pepper
> 6 eggs
> 50 g (2 oz) butter
> 50 g (2 oz) grated Gruyère cheese

Wash the mushrooms if necessary and then slice them finely. Melt the butter and fry the mushrooms until they are brown all over. Then work in the flour. When this has all been absorbed, gradually add the wine and stock, and mix in the mayonnaise, chive and parsley. Add salt and pepper to taste and cook for a further 5 minutes.

Pour into individual ramekins. Break an egg into the

centre of each, melt the remaining butter and pour a little over each egg. Sprinkle with the cheese. Stand the ramekins in a pan of warm water and bake in a fairly hot oven until cooked – about 5 minutes.

SERVES 6.

Egg, Avocado and Sherry Mousse

I find this one of the most delicious ways of starting a meal.

2 avocados – they *must* be ripe
juice of 1 small lemon
6 hard-boiled eggs
salt and pepper
150 ml (¼ pint) good mayonnaise
2 level dessertspoons gelatine
enough water to dissolve it
1 large carton double cream
2 dessertspoons sweet sherry
½ tin anchovies for decoration

Cut the avocados in half, remove the stones, scoop out the flesh and mash it with a stainless-steel fork. Stir in the lemon juice to prevent the flesh changing colour. Use as little as possible.

Shell the eggs and chop them finely. (I always find it easiest to put them in a straight-sided jug and attack them with a knife.) Add salt and pepper to taste and stir in the mayonnaise. Dissolve the gelatine in the water.

Whip the cream in a large bowl until it starts to thicken, then stir in the sherry and gelatine. Add the avocados and the eggs and mix the lot thoroughly. Turn into a straight-sided bowl and leave in a cold place to set. Unmould just before serving, decorate with anchovies and surround with lightly dressed tomato salad.

SERVES 6.

Extra-special Scrambled Eggs

Perhaps shouldn't be served for breakfast; but an unusual variation on a theme.

> 4 eggs
> grated rind of half an orange
> sherry
> salt and pepper
> 1 tablespoon double cream
> 25 g (1 oz) butter
> hot buttered toast

Beat four eggs lightly with a fork and add most of the grated rind, sherry, seasoning and cream. Melt the butter, add the eggs and cook slowly, stirring constantly with a wire whisk, until they achieve a rich creamy consistency. Serve the eggs on hot buttered toast with a little grated orange rind on top.

SERVES 2–3

Grilled Grapefruit

This is a variation on Britain's dullest first course; half a grapefruit with a maraschino cherry in the middle.

> 2 grapefruit
> a little sherry or Madeira
> brown sugar

Halve the grapefruit and prepare in the usual way, loosening all the segments. Sprinkle each half with a little sherry and a thin layer of sugar. Put under a hot grill until the sugar is dissolved and serve immediately.

This can also be served as a pudding.

SERVES 4.

Grapefruit with Gin

You might well think this is an odd combination, but try it and sample its interesting flavour.

> 3 grapefruit
> 6 dessertspoons gin

Prepare the grapefruit ordinarily and pour a dessertspoon of gin over each half. It is unnecessary to add any sugar unless one has a very sweet tooth.

SERVES 6.

Melon Crescents

These make a delicious beginning to a heavy meal.

> 1 honeydew melon
> 300 (11 oz) tin mandarins
> 1 strawberry *or* raspberry jelly
> 3 dessertspoons *or* 1 miniature bottle Grand Marnier
>   (*or* more if feeling especially festive)
> water

Cut the melon in half lengthways and remove seeds. Cut out as many perfect melon balls as possible. With a spoon remove the rest of the flesh (keep this for a fruit salad or the children's supper). Drain the mandarins, reserving the juice. Stand each melon shell on a large piece of foil. Fill them with a mixture of melon balls and mandarins. Mix the Grand Marnier with enough water to make up 275 ml ($\frac{1}{2}$ pint). Pour over jelly cubes in a pan and warm gently until dissolved. Divide the liquid between the two shells, wrap them up and store in the fridge until well set. Cut each piece into three.

SERVES 6.

Mushroom and Chicken Liver Omelette

This filling can be prepared beforehand and kept warm, so all you have to do at the last minute is make the omelette.

    50 g (2 oz) sliced mushrooms
    50 g (2 oz) butter
    1 small shallot
    4 chicken livers
    salt and pepper
    ½ teaspoon flour
    2 tablespoons consommé ⎫ *or* 4 tablespoons
    2 tablespoons white wine ⎭ either one
    2 six-egg omelettes

Sauté the mushrooms in 14 g (½ oz) butter for about 4 to 5 minutes. Remove and keep warm. Chop the shallot finely, slice the chicken livers and fry both in the remaining butter for less than a minute, being careful not to let the livers get hard or the shallot burn. Season well, add the flour and stir for a minute. Then add the consommé and wine. Stir well and add the mushrooms. Keep warm until the omelette is ready.

Make the omelettes, when nearly cooked spread the mixture over one half of the omelettes and fold in the usual way.

SERVES 8 as a starter or 4 for supper.

Mushrooms in Cream

This recipe can also be served as an accompanying vegetable.

    450 g (1 lb) white button mushrooms
    275 ml (½ pint) water
    salt
    275 ml (½ pint) double cream
    2 tablespoons dry white wine
    ground pepper

Wash the mushrooms and remove the stalks. Boil the water with the salt. Add the mushrooms and cook for 3 to 4 minutes. Meanwhile heat the cream in a separate pan together with the wine, do not boil. Drain the mushrooms and add them to the cream. Cook for 2 or 3 minutes and serve immediately with freshly milled black pepper.

SERVES 4.

Chilled Mushroom Cocktail

> 350 g (12 oz) white button mushrooms
> ¼ small onion
> 1 small carton double cream
> 3 tablespoons good mayonnaise
> 2 tablespoons white wine
> 1 tablespoon anchovy essence
> seasoning
> lemon slices

Wash the mushrooms and slice finely. Peel and chop the onion very small. Whip the cream until it thickens.

Make the sauce by mixing together the mayonnaise, cream, onion, wine and anchovy essence. Season well and chill for about 30 minutes. Add the mushrooms and spoon into individual glasses. Chill. Decorate with slices of lemon. Serve with brown bread and butter.

SERVES 4 to 5.

Mushrooms à la Grecque

One of the best cold courses in anybody's repertoire.

> 4 tablespoons oil, preferably olive
> 1 large chopped onion
> 1 crushed clove garlic
> 150 ml (¼ pint) dry white wine

bouquet garni
salt and freshly milled pepper
450 g (1 lb) firm mushrooms
4 peeled and seeded tomatoes
2 tablespoons olive oil.
masses of chopped parsley – at least two handfuls

Heat the oil and fry the onion and garlic until they are soft.
Stir in the wine, bouquet garni, salt and pepper. Peel the
mushrooms and add them to the pan with the tomatoes.
Cook gently for about 15 minutes. Chill. Just before serving, remove bouquet garni and stir in the rest of the oil and
the parsley.

SERVES 4 to 6.

You can make this without the tomatoes, or with a little
lemon juice or with cloves. All just as good.

Orange Vinaigrette

*A refreshing start to a meal. Make in advance but do not
pour vinaigrette over the oranges until the last minute.*

6 large oranges
6 tablespoons olive oil
2 tablespoons wine vinegar
1 teaspoon finely chopped onion
1 good tablespoon orange liqueur
seasoning
1 tablespoon chopped parsley

Peel the oranges, removing all the pith, and slice horizontally. Arrange on a serving dish. Make the dressing by mixing together the oil, vinegar, onion, orange liqueur and
seasoning. Pour over the oranges and sprinkle with parsley.

SERVES 6.

Appetizing Pears

4 ripe pears
Jif lemon juice
4 tablespoons whipped cream
1 tablespoon sherry
125 g (4 oz) cream cheese
1 tablespoon parsley
125 g (4 oz) ham
lettuce leaves

Peel, slice and core the pears. Dip them in lemon juice so that they don't discolour. Whip the cream with the sherry and mix with the cream cheese. Season. Fold in the parsley and finely chopped ham. Pile the mixture on top of the pears and arrange on the lettuce leaves.

SERVES 4 (or 8 if the pears are enormous).

Creamed Spinach with Madeira

This can be served as a separate course or as a vegetable.

900g (2 lb) spinach
¼ cup water
butter
nutmeg
salt and pepper
2 tablespoons double cream
125 g (4 oz) mushrooms
2 tablespoons Madeira
diced white bread

Cook the spinach in water for about 10 minutes or until just soft. Drain thoroughly, squeezing all the water out. Chop into small pieces and once again drain off any excess water. Add 1 tablespoon butter, a little nutmeg, salt and pepper and the cream. Sauté the mushrooms in some butter for a few minutes and add them to the spinach together with the Madeira. Sauté some diced white bread in some butter until the croûtons are golden brown and crisp. Reheat the spinach and sprinkle it with the croûtons before serving.

SERVES 4.

Kipper Pâté

Good, easy, keeps well.

> 1 packet kipper fillets
> 3 tablespoons brandy
> ½ lemon
> 175 g (6 oz) butter

Skin the fillets and leave to soak for an hour or so in the brandy. Melt the butter, squeeze the lemon and put all ingredients in the blender. Switch on. When mixture is smooth turn out into serving dishes. Chill. Serve decorated with thin slices of lemon.

SERVES 4 to 6.

Pork and Liver Pâté

Rich, good and particularly rewarding for smart picnics.

> 225 g (8 oz) calf's liver
> 225 g (8 oz) chicken livers
> 450 g (1 lb) lean pork
> 1 chopped shallot
> 2 tablespoons cinnamon
> 2 tablespoons salt
> 1 tablespoon brandy
> 1 tablespoon Madeira
> 2 tablespoons chopped parsley
> strips of bacon

Mince the livers and the pork until very fine. Add the rest

of the ingredients and mix well together. Line a terrine or loaf tin with strips of bacon and cover with the pâté mixture. Bake in a moderate oven for $1\frac{1}{2}$ to 2 hours. Cool the pâté with a heavy weight on top of it. Chill.

SERVES 8.

It is less effort, and cheaper, to use 675 g (1 lb 8 oz) minced belly pork instead of the lean pork and the strips of bacon. Purists don't, as they like the bacon round the pâté when it is turned out, but it always seems a waste to me as so many people leave the bacon on their plates.

Quick and Easy Chicken Liver Pâté

This is incredibly easy: it takes far longer to wash up than make. Brandy or sherry are the best liquors to use, but in desperation I've used beer reasonably successfully.

    75 g (3 oz) butter
    1 large crushed clove garlic
    $\frac{1}{2}$ small onion
    225 g (8 oz) chicken livers
    3 tablespoons brandy *or* sherry
    1 tablespoon vinegar (optional)
    1 tablespoon French mustard
    salt and pepper

Melt the butter and sauté the garlic and finely chopped onion until transparent. Add the cleaned chicken livers and cook gently for 4 or 5 minutes. Put this in a liquidizer together with the liquor, vinegar, French mustard and seasoning. Turn into a small terrine and leave to cool. Serve with hot toast and butter.

SERVES 4 to 6 depending on one's appetite.

Pheasant Pâté

This is very rich, feeds about 20 people. It is not the quickest recipe in the world but it is not in any way complicated and the finished result is heaven.

> 1 cooked pheasant. You can either roast it or casserole it in a little red wine
> 350 g (12 oz) butter
> 450 g (1 lb) chicken livers
> 1 wineglass brandy
> 1 wineglass sherry
> 4 *or* 5 chopped spring onions (if available)
> 1 tablespoon made mustard

Take the meat off the pheasant which is by far the most fiddly part. Melt half the butter and gently fry the chicken livers until they are pink (about 5 minutes). When the livers are cool put them in a liquidizer, add the rest of the butter and liquidize until smooth. If your machine will stand it put the pheasant through the liquidizer as well, mixed with the liver to act as a lubricant. If your machine is not strong enough, mince the pheasant or chop it finely – the finished result will taste the same but have a different texture. Beat everything vigorously in a large bowl, then put the pâté mixture into the dishes from which it will be served. Keep it in the fridge but do allow it to warm to room temperature for 3 to 4 hours before it is eaten. It will keep for some days in an ordinary fridge.

SERVES 20.

Pâté Mould

An eye-catching way of serving pâté which gives it a Fortnum and Mason look.

> 1 tin consommé
> 1 sherry-glass sherry
> 2 small Philadelphia cream cheeses

225 g (8 oz) good fine pâté (preferably home made) *or*
    2 tins Plumrose pâté de foie gras
2 *or* 3 chopped chives
gelatine if required

Heat the consommé until dissolved, then add the sherry.
Leave to cool. When cool pour a depth of only 1¼ cm (½
inch) into the bottom of the mould and leave in the fridge
until set hard. Mash the cream cheese and pâté with a fork
until the mixture is smooth. Sprinkle the chives on to the
centre of the set consommé. Put the pâté mixture on top of
this leaving 2½ cm (1 inch) free round the edge. Then pour
the rest of the consommé around and over the pâté. Leave
to set in the fridge. Turn out and serve with toast.

SERVES 4 to 6.

If you want to turn this out some time before eating,
dissolve a little gelatine in the consommé at the start.

Pâté de Campagne

*This is my own adaptation of a traditional recipe, as I like
my pâtés more livery than a meat loaf.*

175 g (6 oz) liver *or* even more if you care to
450 g (1 lb) mixed minced veal and pork
125 g (4 oz) minced ham, bacon, beef *or* omit altogether
1 crushed clove (optional)
125 g (4 oz) chopped back pork fat
black pepper
salt – at least 1 teaspoon
bay leaves, parsley, oregano, mace *or* whatever your
    favourite spice happens to be
4 tablespoons wine *or* preferably brandy
piece of flare fat, fatty bacon *or* whatever you can
    cajole from your butcher to cover the pâté while it
    is cooking

Mince, chop or liquidize the liver. Put all the ingredients

into a big bowl and mix them very well. This is the only thing you have to do to make your pâté good. It is worth doing properly or else give up and buy a commercially made pâté which, unless it is very expensive, won't be much good so should inspire you to keep mixing.

If the mixture seems a little dry (which it might, the meat can vary greatly) add some more wine. It shouldn't be sloppy but it won't matter greatly if it is. Pack it in a suitable vessel (at least 675 ml (1½ pint) capacity), cover it well and bake in a moderate oven for about 1½ hours. It may take longer. To see if it is cooked, poke it with a small knife and then press down alongside. If blood runs out keep cooking. Let it cool and preferably keep for a day before eating. Either serve direct from the bowl or turn out and scrape off the fat.

Some people say you should let the mixture stand for an hour or two before cooking – it never seems to make the slightest odds to me so I've given up doing so. If bay leaves are your favourite flavouring, decorate the top of the pâté with them.

This feeds 6 to 8 quite substantially.

Easy Pork and Liver Terrine

Every household should have at least one of these in their freezer or freezer part of the fridge. It's simple, so good, not even fattening.

> 450 g (1 lb) pig's liver
> 125 g (4 oz) belly of pork
> salt and pepper
> 1 clove garlic *or* more to taste
> 2 tablespoons of any wine *or* any spirit except gin *or*, at a pinch, cider
> 1 rasher bacon

Mince liver and pork (or ask your butcher to). Add the seasoning, crushed garlic and wine. Pack it into a 550 ml

(1 pint) terrine or any small suitable ovenproof bowl. Cut the bacon into fine strips and press them on to the mixture. Cover and bake for 1 hour in a medium oven. Then remove cover and bake for a further 10 minutes. Purists stand the terrine in a bowl of water while cooking but it isn't necessary.

SERVES 4 to 6.

Tuna-fish Pâté

If the mercury scare hasn't put you off tuna for ever you could try this easy pâté.

>   175 g (6 oz) butter
>   1 large tin tuna
>   3 tablespoons olive oil
>   juice of a lemon
>   1 small onion
>   3 tablespoons brandy
>   salt and pepper

Melt the butter. Put all the ingredients into a blender and liquidize until smooth. Turn out into serving dishes. Chill.

Ideally take out of the fridge 1 hour before serving. Garnish with chopped hard-boiled eggs, olives, etc.

SERVES 6.

Sardine Pâté

This is similar to the previous recipe. If you double up the quantities and mash the sardines instead of liquidizing them you make a very nice sardine mould which can be served as a main course in the summer with a tomato salad.

>   175 g (6 oz) butter
>   2 tins sardines

3 tablespoons olive oil
juice of a lemon
1 small onion
3 tablespoons sherry
pepper
1 tablespoon parsley

Melt the butter. Put all ingredients except parsley into a
blender and switch on. When smooth stir in the grated
parsley and turn out into a serving dish. Chill. Garnish
with anchovies, chives or what you will.

SERVES 6.

Shrimp Pâté

Another easy first course.

225 g (8 oz) cooked and shelled shrimps
2 tablespoons lemon juice
salt and freshly ground black pepper
a generous pinch of paprika
3 tablespoons sherry
just under half a cup of olive oil

Prepare the shrimps and put in a liquidizer together with
the rest of the ingredients. When smooth turn out and chill
in the fridge. Serve with toast and butter.

SERVES 6.

Smoked-salmon Pâté

*Personally I never enjoy smoked-salmon pâté as much as
smoked salmon, but for people with really jaded palates
this is good. It is also a useful way of using up the scrappy
bits if you've been lucky enough to have had a whole
smoked salmon.*

75 g (3 oz) soft butter
2 tablespoons sherry
225 g (8 oz) smoked salmon
4 tablespoons double cream
pinch of paprika

Put the first three ingredients into a liquidizer and beat until smooth. Then add the cream and paprika. Pour into a serving bowl and keep in the fridge until needed.

SERVES 4 to 6 depending on what follows.

Turkey Pâté

A delicious way of using up the turkey left-overs.

4 walnuts (8 halves or more if cared for)
2 tablespoons sherry
225 g (8 oz) turkey meat
125 g (4 oz) ham
50 g (2 oz) breadcrumbs
275 ml (½ pint) chicken stock
25 g (1 oz) gelatine
seasoning

Marinate the walnuts in the sherry for about 30 minutes. Mince the turkey and ham and mix well with the breadcrumbs. Chop the nuts and add to the mixture. Heat the stock and dissolve the gelatine in it, stirring until it is quite smooth. Let this cool and then add the turkey mixture and blend well. Season to taste. Pour into a 875 ml (1½ pint) basin and put a heavy weight on top. Leave in a cool place. Dip the bowl in warm water, turn out and decorate with cucumber slices or bunches of watercress.

SERVES 6.

Apple Curry Soup

An original recipe which is very popular – I tried it at a time when apples were coming out of my ears in the autumn and I was determined not to serve them as a pudding yet again.

> 25 g (1 oz) butter
> 1 medium-sized onion
> 550 ml (1 pint) chicken stock
> 1 tablespoon curry powder
> 1 tablespoon cornflour
> 150 ml ($\frac{1}{4}$ pint) double cream
> 2 egg yolks
> 2 eating apples
> salt and pepper
> some Jif lemon
> 2 tablespoons Calvados
> a little greenery to garnish

Melt the butter. Chop the onion and cook until golden. Add the stock and curry powder, and the cornflour mixed with a drop of water. Bring to boiling point and simmer for about 10 minutes. Heat the cream and stir in the egg yolks. When smooth stir slowly into the soup.

Pour the soup into a liquidizer and add a peeled and cored apple. Blend until smooth. Add a little salt and pepper to taste and then chill. Just before serving, cut up the remaining apple and sprinkle with lemon juice to stop it turning brown, and add it to the soup with the Calvados. Garnish with a little greenery.

SERVES 4.

Iced Avocado Soup

This is very rich but absolutely delicious.

> 2 ripe avocados
> 1 small carton sour cream *or* fresh cream

    seasoning
    pinch of cayenne
    2 tablespoons dry sherry
    milk
    parsley

Cut the avocados in half, remove the stones and scoop out all the flesh. Mash, mouli or liquidize it. Then mix it with the cream, salt and pepper and a pinch of cayenne. Add the sherry and thin the mixture down with milk to the required consistency. Cover the mixture and chill. Decorate with parsley before serving.

SERVES 6.

Bloody Mary Soup

Marvellous.

    2 tablespoons butter
    1 finely chopped onion
    3 diced sticks celery
    2 tablespoons tomato purée
    1 tablespoon sugar
    5 cups tomato juice
    1 tablespoon salt
    2 teaspoons Worcestershire Sauce
    $\frac{1}{4}$ teaspoon pepper
    a dash of lemon juice
    4 tablespoons vodka

Melt the butter and gently fry the onions and celery until golden brown. Stir in the tomato purée and sugar, add the tomato juice and simmer for 10 minutes. Add the remaining ingredients. Liquidize. This can be served hot or cold.

SERVES 6.

Caviar and Consommé Soup

> 2 tins consommé
> 3 tablespoons sherry
> 1 small pot lumpfish roe (mock caviar)
> sour cream *or* double cream

Melt the consommé and add the sherry and caviar. Pour into individual dishes and leave in the fridge to gel. Serve cold with a dollop of cream on the top.

SERVES 4 to 6.

Iced Cherry Soup

Unusual, light and much liked.

> 150 ml (¼ pint) red wine
> 2 cloves
> pared rind of half an orange
> pinch of cinnamon
> 1 tin black cherries in syrup
> sugar if required
> juice of 1 lemon *or* to taste
> 550 ml (1 pint) water
> 1½ tablespoons cornflour
> sour cream to garnish

Gently simmer the wine, cloves, orange and cinnamon for a few minutes. Strain the wine into a fresh saucepan and add the cherries, syrup, sugar, lemon juice and almost all the water. Bring to the boil.

Meanwhile blend the cornflour with the remaining water and add to the soup. Simmer for about 2 minutes, stirring all the time. Pour into a container and chill. Stir well before serving. Garnish with a dollop of sour cream in each soup dish.

SERVES 4.

Chestnut Cream Soup

Don't be put off by the thought of skinning the chestnuts. This soup is well worth it and is extremely economical.

> 350 g (12 oz) chestnuts (tinned will do but they do not taste as good)
> 875 ml (1½ pints) stock
> 25 g (1 oz) butter
> 50 g (2 oz) flour
> 275 ml (½ pint) milk
> 75 ml (½ gill) sherry
> parsley
> salt and pepper
> a little cream

Slit the chestnuts, and boil in water for about 10 minutes so that the skins come off easily. Peel them – this is the worst part of all, so don't give up, it is well worth it in the end. Put the shelled nuts in a saucepan together with the stock and cover and simmer for 1 hour. Liquidize. Melt the butter and add the flour, then stir in the stock and cook until it boils. Meanwhile, boil the milk and stir it into the soup. (If the chestnuts have been cooked too quickly, it may be too thick, and can be thinned with more boiling milk.) Add the sherry and parsley and season with salt and pepper. A dollop of cream on the top when serving looks and tastes good.

SERVES 6.

Good Vegetable Soup

In winter it pays fantastic dividends to keep a good vegetable soup in the house. This is how to do it.

> 3 onions
> 3 leeks
> 3 sticks celery
> 2 potatoes

125 g (4 oz) butter *or* oil
1 large glass sherry *or* wine
1 large tin tomatoes
more vegetables

Peel and chop the vegetables you plan to include.

Heat the butter and gently fry the vegetables until they soften a little. Then pour on the sherry or wine (or beer or cider) and let it get absorbed by the vegetables. Pour in the tomatoes. Stir well and add a pint or so of cold water. Bring to the boil and simmer gently until the vegetables are soft (1 hour or so).

If your soup is full of large lumps of vegetables, liquidize it. If you prepared the vegetables exhaustively and it looks more like minestrone, don't.

SERVES at least 6.

This is a deliberately vague recipe because you can make it what you will: more carrots and it's basically carrot soup; you can add cauliflower or the better cauliflower leaves; drop in the outer leaves of a lettuce, the left-over mashed potatoes from your kid's supper or virtually any vegetable in the house you want eaten up, or that's cheap and in season at the time. I never thicken this kind of soup as it is quite thick enough for me as it is, and anyway it's more slimming not to, but if you care to you can dissolve flour or cornflour in a little of the liquid and stir it in; but you may well end up having to thin it down with a little water!

Grated cheese sprinkled on top makes it even better.

Cold Comfort

And who could refuse anything with such an evocative name?

1 tin consommé
2 glasses sherry
2 tablespoons fresh double cream
chopped chives
1 chopped hard-boiled egg

Chill the consommé in the fridge for some hours. Fifteen minutes before eating spoon half into each of two bowls. Pour the sherry over and the cream and sprinkle with egg and chives.

SERVES 2.

Curried Cream-cheese Consommé

A very popular recipe which couldn't be easier – serve it in ramekin dishes and it goes further.

> 3 packets Philadelphia cream cheese
> 1½ tins consommé
> curry powder to taste
> salt and pepper
> sherry

Liquidize the cream cheese and 1¼ tins consommé, curry powder, salt and pepper until well blended. Pour into individual ramekin dishes and chill until set. Add some sherry to the remaining consommé – warm through if still jellied, allow to cool and pour over the cream cheese mixture. Chill.

SERVES 8.

Gazpacho

On a hot day thoughts turn to cold soups and this is one of the best.

> 2 cloves garlic
> 1 green pepper
> 1 Spanish onion
> 6 large ripe tomatoes
> ½ cucumber
> 6 tablespoons olive oil
> 2 tablespoons vinegar

2 tablespoons red wine
875 ml (1½ pints) iced water

Liquidize slowly the garlic, half the seeded green pepper, half the onion, 4 skinned and seeded tomatoes, half of the half cucumber, oil, vinegar and wine. Add this to the iced water. Season well with plenty of pepper. Leave to chill.

Chop the remaining cucumber, onion, tomatoes and pepper very finely indeed and put them in separate bowls. If you can be bothered, croûtons are always much appreciated.

SERVES 6.

Orange and Tomato Soup

Simply couldn't be easier to make and the flavour is excitingly unusual.

> 1 packet tomato soup (do not use Heinz, it is too sweet)
> 1 orange
> 2 tablespoons orange liqueur
> 4 tablespoons cream

Make the tomato soup up to 875 ml (1½ pints) with water. Grate the rind of the orange, and add to the soup together with the juice. Simmer for a few minutes. Just before serving add the liqueur. Put a tablespoon of cream into the bottom of each bowl. Pour on the soup.

SERVES 4.

Spinach Soup

> 275 g (10 oz) tin *or* packet spinach purée
> 275 ml (½ pint) cream
> 1 crushed clove garlic
> salt

freshly milled black pepper
2 tablespoons sherry or white wine

Mix all the ingredients well together and chill before serving. (Add some milk if too thick.)

SERVES 4.

Tomato Consommé

2 level tablespoons gelatine
1 chicken stock cube
425 ml ($\frac{3}{4}$ pint) boiling water
550 g (19 oz) tin tomato juice
1 tablespoon Jif lemon
angostura bitters
seasoning
lemon slices
mint freeze:
2 tablespoons finely chopped mint
1 tablespoon Jif lemon
1 bottle low-calorie lemonade

Dissolve the gelatine and stock cube in the boiling water. Add the tomato juice, some Jif lemon and a few drops angostura bitters. Season well. Leave to set in the fridge.

Meanwhile mix together the mint, lemon juice and the lemonade. Pour into an ice tray and freeze to the soft ice stage.

To serve, chop up the tomato jelly and pile into glasses with the mint freeze and lemon slices on top.

SERVES 4 to 6.

Tomato Soup

It is much nicer than commercial tomato soup.

1 large onion
900 g (2 lb) tomatoes
40 g (1½ oz) butter
2 tablespoons flour
2 glasses white wine
1¼ l (2½ pints) good stock
a pinch of thyme
salt and pepper
150 ml (¼ pint) single cream
a few chopped chives

Peel and chop the onion. Peel and dice the tomatoes, not too small. Melt the butter and cook the onions until golden. Add the flour and stir constantly for about 2 minutes. Remove from the heat and add the wine and stock. Return to the stove and add the rest of the ingredients except the cream, cover and simmer for about 1 hour. Liquidize. Reheat before serving in individual bowls with a dollop of cream in the bottom. Sprinkle with chopped chives.

SERVES 6.

Coquilles St Jacques

This is the best recipe that I know for this delicious food, but unless you have a cheap source of scallops it can be very expensive.

12 scallops
2 tablespoons pork dripping *or* olive oil
6 finely chopped shallots *or* 2 small onions
125 g (4 oz) sliced button mushrooms
¼ bottle dry white wine
1 small carton double cream
2 beaten egg yolks
2 slices bread
25 g (1 oz) grated cheese

Wash the scallops and scrub the shells. Cut each white part into three and reserve the orange. Melt the fat and cook the scallops gently for 10 minutes with the shallots, mushrooms and salt and pepper. Meanwhile boil the wine until it is reduced by half. Add this to the scallops with the cream, egg yolks and orange parts. Simmer gently for about 20 minutes until the mixture thickens. Then spoon it into four or six shells. Sprinkle with breadcrumbs and cheese and put under a hot grill until brown.

SERVES 4 to 6, depending on your generosity or your guests' hunger.

Crab Diable

Just the thing to impress a mother-in-law who thinks you can't even boil an egg for her darling son. And it's not much harder.

    1 small onion
    1 shallot
    25 g (1 oz) butter
    2 tablespoons brandy
    1 dessertspoon mustard
    275 ml ($\frac{1}{2}$ pint) white sauce (20 g ($\frac{3}{4}$ oz) butter and
        flour, 275 ml ($\frac{1}{2}$ pint) milk)
    1 large tin crabmeat – drained and flaked
    brown breadcrumbs

Fry the finely chopped onion and shallot in the butter; when golden stir in the brandy and mustard. Make the white sauce, then add the crabmeat and onion mixture. Spoon this into scrubbed scallop shells or ramekins and sprinkle with breadcrumbs. Brown under a hot grill and serve immediately.

SERVES 4 to 6 depending on size of shells.

Crab Mousse

This is a pleasant cold first course, easily made in advance.

1 150 g (5 oz) packet frozen crabmeat, thawed
1 tablespoon lemon juice
cayenne
salt and freshly milled black pepper
1 small carton single cream
2 eggs
1 envelope gelatine
3 tablespoons sherry
parsley to garnish
lemon slices

Mix together the crabmeat, lemon juice and cayenne. Season lightly. Warm the cream in a saucepan and add the egg yolks one by one. Cook gently, stirring all the time until mixture thickens. Dissolve the gelatine in the sherry and add to the cream mixture. Allow to cool a bit and then add the crabmeat. Beat the egg whites until stiff and fold them into the crab mixture. Pour into individual ramekins and chill until serving. Garnish with a little chopped parsley and lemon slices.

SERVES 6.

Kipper Fillets Marinated in White Wine

All working cooks must have a large repertoire of good recipes that not only can be prepared the night before, but are better for it. This is a classic example.

$\frac{1}{2}$ glass dry white wine
4 tablespoons oil
2 tablespoons lemon juice
1 onion, sliced into rings
masses of freshly ground black pepper
3 bay leaves
2 packets kipper fillets – with all black skin peeled off

Mix together the wine, oil, lemon juice, onion, pepper and bay leaves in a dish. Add the kipper fillets and leave to marinate for at least 24 hours in a cool place. The fillets can be drained or served in the juices together with brown bread and butter.

SERVES 6.

Moules Marinières

This is one of my most favourite recipes ever but I only prepare it for people I really love. Whatever experts say, washing, scraping and bearding mussels takes simply hours. So for loved ones ...

> 3–4 l (6–7 pints) mussels
> 25 g (1 oz) butter
> 1 chopped onion *or* 4 chopped shallots
> 275 ml ($\frac{1}{2}$ pint) dry white wine
> salt and pepper
> a sprig of thyme *or* 1 chopped stalk celery
> a handful chopped parsley

Under running water, wash and scrape each mussel and remove the beards. Throw away any that are cracked, open or in any way damaged. Melt the butter in a large pan and fry the onions until soft. Add the wine, salt, pepper, and thyme or celery, with the mussels. Cover and cook over a high heat for about 5 minutes or until all the mussels have opened. Shake the pan from time to time. Take the mussels out of the pan with a slotted spoon and boil the liquid until it is reduced by half. At the last minute add the parsley, pour the liquid over the mussels and serve at once. Really loving cooks remove the one half of each shell while the liquid is reducing. As this is only done in the most expensive restaurants, filled with junior chefs with little else to do, it is not a task I have ever considered essential.

Some people add 275 ml ($\frac{1}{2}$ pint) of double cream with the parsley but I think it spoils the peasanty taste of the meal.

SERVES 6.

Plaice and Mussel Flan

The rich use sole but to my taste it's just as good with plaice.

    225 g (8 oz) shortcrust pastry
    2 shallots *or* ½ small onion
    4 fillets plaice
    50 g (2 oz) butter
    a jar of pickled mussels, well rinsed
    150 ml (¼ pint) dry white wine
    1 large carton single cream
    seasoning

Roll out the pastry until fairly thin; line a 20 cm (8-inch) flan dish. Cover with greaseproof paper weighted down with a few dried beans or peas or something, and bake in a moderate oven for about 20 minutes or until golden brown.

Finely chop the shallots and roll up the fillets. Melt the butter and gently fry the shallots. Then add the fillets, mussels, wine and cream. Season well. Cook for 10 minutes and then remove all the fish. Keep warm. Reduce the sauce by half.

Arrange the fish in the hot flan case (warm through again if necessary as this can be prepared the day before) and pour the sauce on top.

SERVES 4 as a main course, 8 as a starter.

Brandied Prawns with Rice

Expensive first course but more original than boring prawn cocktail.

½ teacup rice
40 g (1½ oz) butter
175 g (6 oz) cooked, shelled prawns,
freshly milled pepper
lemon juice
nutmeg
2 tablespoons brandy
225 g (8 oz) carton double cream
chopped parsley

Cook the rice and keep warm in the oven. Melt the butter and sauté the prawns for a few minutes, having seasoned them with the pepper, lemon juice and nutmeg. Warm the brandy, set alight and pour over the prawns, shaking the pan well. When the flames have gone out, add the cream and let it boil until it thickens, continuously shaking. Put the rice into individual ramekins and pour the prawn mixture on top. Sprinkle with parsley.

SERVES 4.

Whisky Prawns

First class.

¾ teacup rice
50 g (2 oz) butter
2 tablespoons olive oil
1 small onion, chopped
2 cloves garlic, crushed
450 g (1 lb) prawns
2 tomatoes, peeled and seeded
1 sherry-glass whisky
1 sherry-glass wine
75 ml (⅛ pint) double cream
about 2 teaspoons cornflour
seasoning
cayenne

Cook the rice and keep warm. Melt the butter and oil in a pan and fry the onion and garlic until soft. Add the prawns and chopped tomatoes, season well and sauté for a few minutes. Warm half the whisky in a ladle and add to the prawns. Flame, shaking the pan. Pour on the wine and keep on a low heat for about 5 minutes. Remove the prawns and keep on a low heat for about 5 minutes. Remove the prawns and keep warm. Mix together the remaining whisky, cream and cornflour and add to the sauce. Bring to the boil and add a pinch of cayenne, plus some more seasoning if necessary. Serve on individual warmed dishes – a layer of rice with the prawns on top and the sauce poured over.

SERVES 6 to 8.

Prawn and Orange Salad

Not a starter you'll have had hundreds of times. Interesting I think.

> 350 g (12 oz) prawns
> 4 oranges
> 3 tablespoons orange liqueur
> 1 chopped small onion
> juice of ½ lemon
> seasoning
> sugar

Shell the prawns and marinate them in the juice of 1 orange and the liqueur for a couple of hours. Marinate the onion in some lemon juice for about 30 minutes. Slice the remaining oranges and add to the prawns together with the onion. Season well and add as much sugar as you think necessary. Toss before serving with brown bread and butter.

SERVES 6.

Salmon Mousse

Tinned salmon is not my most favourite food but the combination of ingredients in this recipe really tastes good.

> 1 fairly large cucumber
> 50 g (2 oz) gelatine
> 2 225 g (8 oz) tins salmon
> 1 tablespoon sherry
> salt and pepper
> 150 ml ($\frac{1}{4}$ pint) evaporated milk
> a little French dressing

Cut one quarter off the cucumber and put it in a poly-thene bag in the fridge. Peel and seed the rest. Boil it in a little water until it is soft and drain it, reserving the water. Dissolve the gelatine in a cup of the cucumber water. Liquidize the drained salmon, cucumber, gelatine, sherry, salt and pepper. Whip the evaporated milk in a large bowl until as stiff as possible. Fold the salmon mixture into it. Pour into a wetted mould and leave in the fridge overnight. Turn it out a couple of hours before serving and decorate with the remaining cucumber which has been finely sliced and marinated in a little French dressing.

SERVES 6.

Scallops Newburg

A rich beginning to a memorable meal.

> 2 tablespoons butter
> 8 cleaned scallops
> a dash of Jif lemon
> 1 dessertspoon flour
> 1 small carton double cream
> 2 tablespoons sherry
> salt and cayenne pepper
> a little greenery

Melt half the butter. Cut the scallops in half and simmer in the butter for a few minutes. Add the lemon juice and simmer for another minute or two. Make a roux out of the remaining butter and the flour, add the cream and bring almost to the boil. Add the sherry, seasoning, scallops and warm through well, being careful not to boil. Pour into individual ramekins and garnish with a little greenery. Serve with brown bread and butter.

SERVES 4.

Shellfish Summer

    2 tablespoons butter
    1 onion
    1 tablespoon tomato purée
    salt and freshly milled black pepper
    1 tablespoon sugar
    1 tablespoon chopped parsley
    1 tablespoon flour
    2 glasses white wine
    12 cooked scampi
    350 g (12 oz) whole button mushrooms
    2¼ l (2 quarts) mussels
    some Jif lemon juice
    a little greenery to garnish
    boiled rice

Melt the butter and sauté the chopped onion until golden. Add the tomato purée, salt, pepper, sugar and parsley. Simmer briefly. Stir in the flour, add the wine and cook for about 15 minutes. Add the scampi, mushrooms and mussels. Cook until tender. Sprinkle with some Jif lemon and parsley and serve with rice.

SERVES 4 to 6.

Shrimp and Mushroom Appetizer

> 225 g (8 oz) button mushrooms
> 225 g (8 oz) potted shrimps
> lemon juice
> cayenne *or* curry powder
> 3 tablespoons sherry
> 4 slices plain toast
> greenery to garnish

Slice the mushrooms and put in a saucepan with the shrimps and cook over a low heat for about 3 minutes. (Usually there is ample butter in the potted shrimps.) Add the rest of the ingredients, stir and heat. Pour on to the hot toast and sprinkle with parsley.

SERVES 4.

Tuna Ramekins

A remarkably good starter despite the odd mixture of ingredients. Make it in the morning for greater convenience in the evening.

> 4 eggs
> 1 225 g (8 oz) tin tuna fish
> 1 heaped tablespoon arrowroot
> 150 ml (¼ pint) white wine
> 1 tin Campbell's condensed mushroom soup
> 1 large packet of crisps

Hard boil the eggs. Drain and flake the fish. Dissolve the arrowroot in the wine in a large pan. Stir in the soup and heat. Coarsely chop the eggs and add to the pan with the fish. Crush the crisps and add half to the mixture. Divide between the ramekins. Allow to cool. Sprinkle the tops with the remaining crisps and heat through before serving.

SERVES 6 to 8 depending on the size of the ramekins.
(This can also be served in one larger dish, as a main supper course, with a salad.)

Main Dishes

Beef Stroganoff

*Well cooked, this is one of my very most favourite dishes.
For years I cooked it but rarely, believing that it would
only work with top-quality fillet. My local butcher told me
that that simply wasn't true and that any good-quality frying steak would do. Now that the whole process is cheaper
I do it more often.*

675 g (1 lb 8 oz) good-quality frying steak
75 g (3 oz) butter
1 small onion, chopped as finely as possible
225 (8 oz) finely sliced button mushrooms
salt, pepper and paprika
1 tablespoon brandy
1 tablespoon sherry
1 carton sour cream
little lemon juice to taste

First remove every scrap of fat and gristle from the steak.
Then cut it into as fine strips as you have time for. Meanwhile melt the butter, fry the onion until it is transparent,
and then add the mushrooms. When all is cooked remove
the vegetables and keep warm. Add a little more butter if
necessary and fry the meat for the minimum possible time
(it depends on the size of your strips). Sprinkle fairly
lavishly with salt, pepper and paprika, return the vegetables
and pour in the brandy and sherry. Shake the pan briskly
for a moment or two, stir in the cream and a very little
lemon juice. Serve with rice or noodles as soon as the
cream is hot but not boiling.

SERVES 4 to 5.

Chilli con Carne

*As, strictly speaking, this should be served with beans and
rice it is very filling indeed.*

675 g (1 lb 8 oz) beef, minced *or* not
225 g (8 oz) pork, minced *or* not

2 tablespoons oil
2 onions
3 cloves garlic
550 ml (1 pint) red wine
2 tablespoons chilli powder
1 tablespoon cornflour
oregano
bay leaf
pinch cayenne
pinch paprika
salt and pepper
red kidney beans

Either use the mince or remove the fat from the meat and cut it into extremely small bite-size cubes. Take your choice. In any event, heat the oil and fry the sliced onions and chopped garlic until transparent. Then add the meat and fry until brown. Pour on the wine, and bring to the boil. Dissolve the chilli powder in a little water together with the cornflour and add to the casserole. It is difficult to be exact on the quantity of chilli to use. Find out from your grocer just how strong his particular brand is and use it accordingly. Some palates are a whole lot tougher than others so know your friends. Add the rest of the seasonings and cook gently, either in or on the oven, until the meat is tender. This should take just over an hour if it is minced or nearly twice as long if it isn't. Serve with red kidney beans, one tin should be enough for 6.

SERVES 6 or more.

Very Easy Cottage Pie

I don't like cold meat turned into cottage pie but made this way with fresh meat it's no work and tastes infinitely better.

1 tablespoon oil
450 g (1 lb) minced beef
1 chopped onion

1 clove crushed garlic
dash of vinegar
1 small tin tomato paste
2 glasses inferior sherry *or* red wine
salt and pepper
mashed potatoes
grated cheese

Heat the oil and fry the meat until it is brown. Stir in the chopped onion and garlic if you care for it. Cook until the onion is transparent and then stir in a dash of vinegar and the tomato paste. Add the sherry or wine and simmer for about 30 minutes. Keep the meat moist but not runny – either by adding more wine or water or stock.

When cooked put in a casserole, cover with mashed potatoes (instant is acceptable if not sensational), sprinkle with cheese, dot with butter and bake in a hot oven for 10 minutes or a slow oven for 30 minutes.

SERVES 4.

Very Easy Lasagne

Use exactly the same recipe and method as for the cottage pie – omitting, of course, the mashed potatoes.

350 g (12 oz) lasagne
275 ml ($\frac{1}{2}$ pint) strong cheese sauce
red wine
grated cheese

Cook the lasagne according to instructions on packet – probably boil for 15 minutes in salted water. Butter a casserole generously – layer with lasagne, cheese sauce, meat thinned with a little more red wine and continue until ingredients are used up. End with a cheese-sauce layer. Sprinkle with cheese and cook in a moderate oven for 30 minutes.

SERVES 8.

You can add extra layers of carrots, courgettes or celery if you care to.

Very Easy Moussaka

Use the same recipe and method for the meat.

>   900 g (2 lb) aubergines
>   oil
>   red wine
>   275 ml ($\frac{1}{2}$ pint) cheese sauce

Finely slice the aubergines and sprinkle them with salt. Leave to sweat for about 30 minutes or more. Wipe the salt and water off them with absorbent paper. Heat the oil and fry the aubergines, turning once until they are brown and transparent. As each lot are cooked, drain them well on absorbent paper.

Thin the meat mixture with a glass or so of red wine. Butter a casserole and layer it with all the ingredients. Cover and cook for 30 minutes in a moderate oven – uncovering for the last 10 minutes.

SERVES 6 to 8.

Spaghetti Bolognese

This is capable of infinite variations, all good, and is certainly a cheap way of feeding lots of people. Especially useful for feeding friends who help paint your house, dig your garden or turn out your garage, i.e. it takes a short time to prepare and then cooks happily for some time itself.

>   olive oil
>   125 g (4 oz) streaky bacon
>   2 onions
>   1 or 2 cloves garlic, crushed
>   1 stick celery
>   450 g (1 lb) beef mince
>   2 tablespoons tomato paste

1 150 g (5 oz) tin tomatoes
1 seeded and finely chopped green pepper
425 ml (¾ pint) red *or* white wine
275 ml (½ pint) beef stock (made with cube)
salt and masses of pepper
little nutmeg
basil tarragon, thyme *or* bay leaves to taste
thickening if desired
spaghetti
grated Parmesan

Cut the rind off the bacon and snip it up into tiny pieces.
Heat the olive oil, fry the bacon and then add chopped
onions, garlic and celery. When they are lightly browned
remove them. Add a little more oil if necessary and fry the
mince until it ceases to be at all red. Then stir in the bacon,
onions, tomato paste, tomatoes, pepper, stock, wine and
seasonings that you like. Stir from time to time and simmer
for a good hour. Cook spaghetti, pour sauce over and serve,
offering grated Parmesan separately.

SERVES 6 to 8.
Should extra people need to be fed, thicken the sauce with
cornflour and add more wine or stock. Be extra generous
with the cheese.

ROAST MEAT WITH A DIFFERENCE

An extremely pleasant way of roasting any meat is to baste
it with wine. If the meat, be it beef, lamb, poultry or
cracklingless pork, is fat free, first heat a little oil with
herbs, salt, garlic if liked, and a little wine. Pour this over
the meat and roast in the usual way. From time to time
instead of basting with just the existing pan juices, baste
with a tablespoon or so of fresh wine. When the joint is
cooked, remove it into a serving dish and skim off all
excess fat from the pan juices. Do this by allowing the
pan to cool, after which it becomes easy to remove the fat,
by using a spoon, suction syringe device or even rolled-up
pieces of absorbent paper. Make the sauce by stirring cornflour into remaining pan juices, adding another glassful of

wine (or more depending on how many you plan to feed)
and boiling vigorously. Taste and season as needs must.
Stir in some cream just before serving. If the joint is fatty
omit the oil at the start.

GRILLED STEAK WITH VARIOUS SAUCES

So long as you can afford good steak you need never be
without delicious meals. Absolute beginners grill or fry
their steaks until they learn how to cook them to suit them-
selves. The slightly ambitious learn to mash chives, parsley,
garlic or anchovy into butter and put dabs of that on top
of cooked steak. The more ambitious look for something
more challenging.

Here are five sauces which are easy to prepare, good to
eat and produce something of a connoisseur's delight.

Red Wine Sauce

>   14 g (½ oz) butter
>   1 small chopped onion
>   14 g (½ oz) flour
>   ¼ bottle red wine
>   1 small tin tomatoes (or 4 peeled, seeded and chopped
>   tomatoes)
>   1 tablespoon sweet sherry, port or Madeira
>   1 or 2 crushed cloves garlic
>   dash of tomato purée
>   bay leaf
>   salt and pepper

Melt the butter, gently fry the onion. Stir in the flour for 1
minute. Add the wine. Bring to the boil. Add the rest of the
ingredients. Turn down the heat. Cover and simmer for 15
minutes. Remove the bay leaf before serving.

SERVES 4.

Rich Chilled Sauce

275 ml ($\frac{1}{2}$ pint) double cream
1$\frac{1}{2}$ tablespoons brandy
$\frac{1}{2}$ chopped onion
2 tablespoons tomato ketchup
1$\frac{1}{2}$ tablespoons French mustard or pickles
3 tablespoons mayonnaise
dash of Jif lemon juice
seasoning

Whip the cream until very stiff and add the rest of the ingredients. Chill until ready to serve.

SERVES 4.

Mushroom and Brandy Sauce

50 g (2 oz) butter
125 g (4 oz) button mushrooms
dash of lemon juice
2 tablespoons brandy
4 chicken livers
1 *or* 2 tablespoons horseradish sauce
1 small carton single cream

Melt the butter. Gently fry the whole mushrooms just until they are no longer raw. Add the lemon juice. Shake the pan vigorously. Pour in the brandy, light it, shake again. Remove the mushrooms from the pan and keep warm. Meanwhile chop the livers minutely. Fry in the same pan adding a little more butter if necessary. When just cooked (don't overdo them if possible) stir in horseradish to suit your taste. Then add mushrooms and cream and warm through. Don't boil.

SERVES 4.

Bordelaise Sauce

> 150 ml ($\frac{1}{4}$ pint) red wine
> 1 chopped shallot *or* $\frac{1}{2}$ small chopped onion
> marjoram
> thyme
> bay leaf
> salt and pepper
> 150 ml ($\frac{1}{4}$ pint) beef stock
> dash of lemon juice
> 3 to 4 sprigs of parsley, chopped
> 25 g (1 oz) butter

Simmer the wine with the shallot, herbs and seasoning. When it has reduced to a half, add the stock. Continue to cook until it has again reduced to a half. Then add the lemon juice. Strain and add the butter.

SERVES 4.

Mustard and Wine Sauce

Delicious.

> 25 g (1 oz) butter
> 1 small chopped onion
> 425 ml ($\frac{3}{4}$ pint) dry white wine
> 1 tablespoon mild mustard – French *or* Swiss
> handful chopped parsley
> salt and pepper

Melt the butter and gently fry the onion until it is transparent. Stir the wine into the mustard until it is smooth and then pour it into the pan with the parsley, salt and pepper. Simmer gently for 10 minutes. Either pour the sauce over the steak or serve it separately.

SERVES 4.

Bœuf en Daube à la Marseille

Another dish which can be made way in advance and heated up at the last minute – the longer it cooks the better it gets.

900 g (2 lb) good stewing steak
275 ml (½ pint) red wine
2 tablespoons olive oil
ground black pepper
bouquet garni
2 cloves crushed garlic
125 g (4 oz) onions
125 g (4 oz) onions
175 g (6 oz) streaky bacon
1 medium tin tomatoes
12 stoned black olives (green will do)

Cut the steak into bite-size pieces. Put into a large bowl and add the marinade: the wine, oil, black pepper, herbs, garlic and chopped onions and carrots. Stir and leave overnight in a cool place.

Later cut the bacon into strips and line the bottom of a 1½-litre (3-pint) casserole with half of it. Then add the meat and marinade, together with the tomatoes. Sprinkle with the rest of the bacon. Cover and cook as slowly as your oven will for at least 4 hours – ideally 6 or more. Add the olives 30 minutes before serving. If the stew looks fatty skim off any excess.

SERVES 6.

Bœuf en Daube

This is quicker – there is no marinating – but I don't like it quite as much as the previous recipe.

675 g (1 lb 8 oz) good braising beef
1 tablespoon olive oil
4 slices bacon

1 *or* 2 sliced onions
1 *or* 2 crushed cloves of garlic
salt and pepper
bouquet garni
275 ml (½ pint) cheap red wine

Cut the beef into bite-size pieces. Heat the oil and add the chopped bacon. When the fat is transparent add the onions and garlic. When they are soft add the meat, plenty of salt and pepper, the bouquet garni and the wine. Bring to the boil.

Cover the casserole and bake it for at least 3 hours in a slow oven.

Except for cutting up the meat and waiting for the stew to come to the boil this is fast and it couldn't be simpler. It is an ideal meal to make in the early morning and put in an automatic oven so as to be ready for your return.

SERVES 4 to 5.

'Left-over' Stew

This is an excellent way of using up any cold meat. It works equally well with lamb, beef, chicken, ham or turkey. Particularly turkey. So good is it that it is more than likely that when it appears on December 28 your family won't even recognize the turkey. Hopefully.

3 tablespoons oil
2 *or* 3 onions
1 *or* 2 cloves garlic
1 400 g (14 oz) tin tomatoes
1 tablespoon tomato purée
275 ml (½ pint) red *or* white wine
450 g (1 lb) any cooked meat *or* suitable mixture, say
    turkey and ham
bouquet garni
bay leaf
salt and pepper

125 g (4 oz) mushrooms
1 sliced, seeded, green pepper
1 tin corn off the cob (optional)

Heat the oil and fry the roughly chopped onion and crushed
garlic. When transparent stir in the tomatoes and tomato
purée. Pour in the wine and bring to the boil. Add the diced
meat and simmer for 30 minutes with the bouquet garni,
bay leaf and salt and pepper. Add the mushrooms and the
sliced, seeded pepper and cook for a further 15 minutes.
Just before serving you can add a drained tin of corn off the
cob. (N.B. Remove the bouquet garni and bay leaf before
serving.)

SERVES 4.

Bœuf au Grand Marnier

1 orange
675 g (1 lb 8 oz) braising beef
275 ml (½ pint) red wine
150 ml (¼ pint) beef stock
4 crushed juniper berries *or* 1 tablespoon redcurrant
    jelly
bouquet garni
225 g (8 oz) onions, sliced
1–2 crushed cloves garlic
cooking oil
1 tablespoon flour
2–3 tablespoons Grand Marnier
salt and pepper

Finely peel the orange. Remove white pith from the peel
and cut the peel into thin shreds. Store in an air-tight container. Squeeze the juice out of the orange.

Remove all fat from the meat and cut into cubes.
Marinate the meat overnight in the orange juice, wine,
stock, fruit, bouquet garni, onions, garlic, salt and pepper.

Drain, reserving the marinade. Heat oil and fry the meat
in it until it is brown. Stir in the flour, add the marinade and

orange peel and bring to the boil. Reduce heat and simmer
for 2 hours. Then taste and add more seasoning if necessary. Add the Grand Marnier, cook a few minutes longer
and serve.

SERVES 4.

Mother-in-Law's Hot Pot

So called because it's made with stout and bitter.

> 900 g (2 lb) beef
> 4 onions
> 4 carrots
> 900 g (2 lb) potatoes
> seasoning
> equal quantities of stout and bitter (about 150 ml ($\frac{1}{4}$
> pint) each)

Remove all the fat from the steak and cut it into cubes.
Slice the onions into fine rings, the carrots into rounds and
the potatoes into slightly thicker rounds. Then pack the
meat and vegetables in layers into a casserole ending with
a potato layer. Season well. Pour in enough beer to fill two-
thirds of the casserole. Bake covered in a moderate oven
for 2 hours – then uncovered for a further 30 minutes.
Should the hot pot look as if it might dry out, add more
beer.

SERVES 6.

Brown-ale Stew

Perfect for a cold day.

> 40 g ($1\frac{1}{2}$ oz) dripping
> 675 g ($1\frac{1}{2}$ lb) braising beef
> 6 large onions
> 2 cloves garlic

seasoning
1 tablespoon brown sugar
1 tablespoon flour
550 ml (1 pint) brown ale
slices French bread
mustard

Melt the dripping in an iron casserole dish. Cut the meat into
2½-cm (1-inch) cubes and brown quickly in the fat. Remove
the meat from the casserole and brown the onions quickly,
stirring all the time. Remove any excess fat and replace
the meat in the casserole together with the crushed garlic,
brown sugar and flour. Cook for about 3 minutes, stirring
constantly and add the ale. Season. Bring to the boil and
cook slowly for a couple of hours.

About 20 minutes before serving, remove any excess fat
and pour it over the French bread previously coated with
mustard. Put the bread on top of the casserole and put in
a hot oven or under the grill for about 15 minutes or until
the bread is brown and crisp.

SERVES 4.

Bœuf en Croûte

*This is delicious, easy and never fails to impress your
guests who always imagine that you must be brilliant. You
should use fillet but having an enormously reliable butcher
who will provide me excellent cheaper alternatives, I never
do go to such expense.*

900 g (2 lb) beef of good roasting quality
butter
pepper
125 g (4 oz) chopped mushrooms
2 chopped slices not too fatty bacon
1 chopped onion
1 glass red wine
chopped mixed herbs
parsley

225 g (8 oz) frozen puff pastry
egg *or* milk for glazing

Take any fat off the meat and tie the joint into a cylindrical shape. Ideally get your butcher to do it (this will not be successful if your meat comes in a net).

Melt some of the butter, pepper the meat and fry it in the butter until it is brown all over. Put it in a hot oven for 10 minutes. Allow the meat to cool. Cook the chopped mushrooms, bacon and onion in the red wine until they are soft, add the herbs and allow to cool.

Roll the pastry into a rectangle and cut off about a third. Put the drained vegetable mixture into the middle of the larger piece with the meat on top. Fit the pastry around the meat and put the smaller piece on top as lid. Pinch them together, glaze with egg or milk, decorate with bits of pastry if you have the inclination and bake in a hot oven for about 30 minutes, depending on how rare you like your beef. This can be served cold but to my taste it is infinitely nicer hot.

SERVES 4 or more.

Beef with Anchovies and Port

This is very subtle.

6 tablespoons cooking oil
4 chopped onions
900 g (2 lb) good stewing steak
seasoned flour
1 tin anchovies, drained
12 olives
½ wineglass port
550 ml (1 pint) good stock
seasoning
a little parsley to garnish

Heat the oil and sauté the onions until golden and put into a casserole. Cut the meat into cubes, roll in the seasoned flour and fry in the oil until the juices are sealed. Add to the casserole plus the chopped anchovies (use kitchen scissors), stoned olives, the port and stock. Season well. Cook in a slow oven for about 2½ hours until meat is tender. Garnish with a little parsley before serving.

SERVES 6.

Cheese Fondue

A very simple dish to prepare – but one does need a fondue set for serving.

> 1 clove garlic
> 125 g (4 oz) cheese per person (equal quantities Gruyère and Emmental if possible)
> 150 g (5 oz) Fendant, Neuchâtel *or* dry white wine per head
> 3 teaspoons cornflour per head
> 1 liqueur-glass Kirsch per head
> pepper
> nutmeg
> diced bread

Rub a pan with the cut clove of garlic, add the cheese and wine. Cook over medium heat for about 4 minutes. Turn down heat. Mix the cornflour and Kirsch and pour it into the cheese, boil gently, still stirring. Season with pepper and nutmeg. Serve with diced bread.

Winged Victory

A very simple and yet extremely good recipe for a cosy dinner à deux.

> ½ finely chopped onion
> 2 teaspoons chopped thyme
> salt and freshly milled black pepper
> 1 poussin

rosemary
2 bay leaves
a little butter
2 glasses dry white wine *or* cider

Put some of the onion, thyme and salt inside the bird, put rosemary under the wings and fit the bay leaves under the wings to look like a victory sign. Season well and cover with dollops of butter. Put the poussin in a baking dish and sprinkle the remaining onion round the edge. Cover with the wine and place in a fairly hot oven for about 45 minutes, basting and turning about every 15 minutes. If the wine evaporates, add more.

SERVES 2.

Chicken San Marco

I always welcome any chicken recipe which is not in the usual white sauce – and here is one which is quick and easy.

4 chicken joints
seasoning
50 g (2 oz) plain flour
2 tablespoons corn oil
425 ml (¾ pint) white sauce
1 small tin mandarin oranges
good pinch of tarragon
1 tablespoon orange liqueur
50 g (2 oz) chopped roasted almonds

Skin the chicken pieces and roll them in the seasoned flour. Heat the oil and brown the chicken pieces quickly. Make the white sauce with a roux and chicken stock and add the strained juice from the oranges. Pour over the chicken and cook in a casserole dish for about 45 minutes in a moderate oven. Remove from the oven, add the liqueur and the drained mandarin oranges and stir to mix well. Sprinkle with the chopped, roasted almonds and serve.

SERVES 4.

Echoes of the Raj

Chicken is cheap, brandy and cream aren't but the finished result is simply produced and tastes superb.

    3 tablespoons oil
    3 tablespoons butter
    3 large chopped onions
    4 teaspoons curry powder
    1 large jointed chicken
    whole peppercorns
    salt
    1 sherry-glass brandy
    275 ml ($\frac{1}{2}$ pint) double cream

Heat the oil and butter and fry the onions, covered, until they are soft. Stir in the curry powder, arrange the chicken on the onions and cover. Season. Cook gently for about 30 minutes, turning the chicken occasionally. Pour in the brandy and cream and cook for a further 5 minutes. Serve at once or keep warm on a very low heat.

If this dish is to be frozen, add the brandy and cream before serving.

SERVES 6.

Chicken Quarters in Sherry and Cream

This can be made on a gas ring in a bedsitter and is infinitely preferable to plain fried chicken.

    2 chicken quarters
    salt and pepper
    a little flour
    50 g (2 oz) butter
    3 shallots *or* 1 small onion
    225 g (8 oz) button mushrooms
    $\frac{1}{2}$ glass sherry
    $\frac{1}{2}$ glass white wine
    1 small carton cream

Dip the chicken pieces in the seasoned flour. Heat the butter and fry the chicken for about 15 minutes in a covered pan. Don't let it burn. Remove the chicken and keep warm. Add the finely chopped shallots and most of the mushrooms, chopped, to the pan. Fry gently until the shallots are transparent. Then pour off any excess fat. Add the sherry and wine to the pan, scrape up the bits off the bottom and stir well. Add the cream and heat until it simmers. Season to taste and pour the sauce over the chicken. Garnish with the remaining whole mushrooms and asparagus tips if available.

SERVES 2.

If your local greengrocer sells nice cheap mushroom stalks use them instead and strain the sauce before pouring it over the chicken.

Chicken with Whisky

Very good and much enjoyed.

> 3 tablespoons butter
> 1 tablespoon French mustard
> the juice of $\frac{1}{2}$ lemon
> salt and pepper
> 4 chicken quarters
> 1 tablespoon butter
> 1 glass whisky
> 1 glass fresh cream

Work the softened butter, mustard, lemon juice, salt and pepper into a paste and spread it over the chicken.

Melt the remaining butter in a casserole and brown the chicken all over. Cover and cook gently for 30 minutes.

Pour the whisky over the chicken. Allow it to warm for a moment and set it alight. Pour the cream into the casserole, and cook gently, without boiling, for 10 minutes.

SERVES 4.

Chicken Quarters in White Wine and Tarragon Sauce

Another method of cooking boring chicken quarters and can be done even if the cooking facilities are no more sophisticated than a gas ring.

4 chicken pieces
seasoned flour
50 g (2 oz) butter
3 sliced onions
1 tablespoon tomato purée
pinch of thyme
½ bottle of white wine
dash of tabasco
few sprigs tarragon *or* 1 tablespoon dried tarragon
sprinkled with a little white wine

Dip the chicken quarters in flour. Melt the butter and fry the chicken gently until brown all over. Add the onions, put a lid on the pan and leave to simmer for 10 minutes. Stir in the tomato purée and thyme and gradually add the wine. Simmer gently until the chicken is tender (about 30 minutes). Five minutes before serving, stir in tabasco and tarragon.

SERVES 4, or 5 if another piece of chicken is added.

Roast Chicken with Tarragon and Wine

A variation on the now classic method of roasting chicken with lemon and butter.

1 chicken
1 lemon
125 g (4 oz) butter
fresh *or* dry tarragon (if dry, soak in lemon juice *or* white wine first)
1 glass white wine *or* sherry
2 tablespoons double cream

Cut a lemon in half and squeeze the juice. Put the two halves inside the bird, together with half the butter and the tarragon. Pour the juice inside the bird. Then roast it in the remaining butter in a fairly hot oven for at least 45 minutes, turning from time to time. Put it on a carving dish and keep warm.

Meanwhile pour the wine into the pan and scrape in everything. When all is well mixed stir in the cream. Serve the sauce separately.

SERVES as many as the bird feeds. If it is large, increase the quantities for the sauce.

Boned Chicken in Wine

Marks and Spencer now sell ready-boned chickens bound in nets. They are excellent and though they seem expensive, there is practically no waste. This recipe I evolved when they first appeared and find that it is much liked. It takes longer to read than do.

2 tablespoons olive oil
1 boned chicken (450 g (1 lb) or just over)
125 g (4 oz) button mushrooms
275 ml (½ pint) dry white wine
freshly ground black pepper
1 teaspoon arrowroot
2 tablespoons sour cream

Heat the oil and fry the chicken in as small a casserole as possible. Keep turning until it is brown all over. Meanwhile peel the mushrooms if necessary, but do not slice them. Pack them round the chicken and pour in the wine. Bring to the boil and cook in a hot oven for 30 to 45 minutes. Then remove the chicken, take off the net and slice it on to a serving dish. Keep warm. Meanwhile boil the sauce vigorously to reduce it by a third. Taste it, it may need salt but as the chicken is ready-salted it may not. Sprinkle in some pepper. Stir in the arrowroot and heat a little longer. Stir in the cream and pour the sauce over the chicken.

SERVES 3 to 4.

Coq au Vin

This simplified version of the French classic is simple to prepare, fairly quick and can be done a day in advance if need be.

> 2 tablespoons olive oil
> 1–2 cloves garlic
> 6 small onions
> 1 chicken cut into pieces
> ½ bottle red wine
> bouquet garni
> 1 *or* 2 bay leaves
> seasoning
> oil *or* butter
> 1 tablespoon butter
> 2 tablespoons flour
> 125–175 g (4–6 oz) button mushrooms

Heat the oil and gently fry the crushed garlic and onions. When they are fairly soft add the giblets and wing tips. When these are brown add the red wine, herbs and seasoning. Bring to the boil and simmer for a couple of hours.

Meanwhile fry the chicken pieces in either oil or butter. They should be fairly well cooked. Put them in a casserole. Mash the butter and flour together. When the stock is cooked take out the onions and add them to the casserole together with the peeled mushrooms. Strain the rest of the sauce on to the butter and flour thickening and pour over the chicken. This can all be done the day or morning before your dinner party.

When you want the *coq au vin*, heat it up in a medium-hot oven for 30 minutes. Don't leave it in too long or the flesh starts coming off the bones which isn't pretty. The sauce is so good it does need bread, potatoes or rice to ensure you can eat it all.

SERVES 4 to 6 depending on how the chicken has been cut.

Chicken in Port

Which is a change from coq au vin *and much easier.*

> 2 tablespoons oil
> 2 tablespoons butter
> 1 large chopped onion
> a generous quantity of chopped parsley
> 1 large jointed chicken
> 2 wineglasses port
> seasoning
> a little arrowroot
> fried bread triangles
> watercress

Heat the oil and butter and fry the onion and parsley in a covered pan. When soft add the chicken and port. Season well. Cover and cook till tender which should be in 30 minutes. Thicken the sauce with a little arrowroot and arrange in a deep serving dish. Garnish with fried bread triangles and watercress.

SERVES 6.

Italian Chicken-liver Flan

A variation on the quiche lorraine theme of which I am very fond. It makes an excellent light supper dish served with a salad.

> 50 g (2 oz) butter
> 225 g (8 oz) chicken livers, cleaned and sliced
> seasoning
> 50 g (2 oz) sliced mushrooms

1 sherry-glass Marsala
3 eggs
125 g (4 oz) double cream *or* evaporated milk
1 baked flan case
Parmesan

Melt the butter and fry the livers until they are delicately pink inside. That's when they stop oozing blood. Be liberal with the salt and pepper. Remove them with a slotted spoon and fry the mushrooms in the remaining butter. Remove them after 10 minutes. Pour in the Marsala and stir well. Meanwhile beat the eggs and cream. Stir the livers, mushrooms and pan juices into this mixture. Pour it all into the flan case, sprinkle with Parmesan and bake in a fairly hot oven until golden (about 20 minutes).

SERVES 4.

Chicken Mousse

An excellent summer dinner dish, particularly delicious with new potatoes, or as part of a cold buffet. Little effort.

1½ tablespoons gelatine
150 ml (¼ pint) chicken stock
150 ml (¼ pint) white wine
1 sliced tomato
1 sliced green pepper } *or* olives *or* cucumber
450 g (1 lb) cooked chicken, diced (1 medium-size chicken)
125 g (4 oz) ham, diced
1 small carton double *or* sour cream
seasoning

Dissolve the gelatine in the chicken stock, add the wine and chill. Pour a little of the liquid in the bottom of a straight-sided mould and arrange the vegetables in a pretty pattern. Leave to set in the fridge. Mix the chicken, ham and cream together with seasoning and the remaining liquid and pour on top of the mould. Leave to set in the fridge. Unmould just before serving.

SERVES 6.

Ham Braised with Madeira

This is always popular, the sweetness of the Madeira likes the saltiness of the ham which in turn is vastly improved by the spinach. One of my favourites.

> 900 g (2 lb) piece of bacon *or* ham
> 1 tablespoon oil
> 4 tablespoons Madeira *or* sweet sherry
> 2 carrots
> 1 largish onion
> 1 stick celery
> 1 bouquet garni
> pepper and salt
> 425 ml (¾ pint) beef stock (cube will do)
> 1 large packet frozen spinach
> grated nutmeg
> 150 ml (¼ pint) single cream
> arrowroot to thicken
> 2 more tablespoons Madeira

Soak the bacon overnight if necessary (i.e. don't if it is a sweetcure boil-in-the-bag variety). Heat the oil in a casserole and gently fry the bacon, turning from time to time until all of it has been in contact with the heat. Pour in the Madeira and try to light it – you may not be successful but not to worry. Remove the bacon and add the chopped vegetables. Cover and leave on a low heat for a few minutes. When the vegetables have started to go transparent replace the bacon on top of them, add the bouquet garni, masses of pepper and the stock. Bring to the boil and either simmer for an hour or so or bake in a medium oven.

Just before the meat is cooked put the still-frozen spinach in a pan on a medium heat. Stir when it becomes possible.

When cooked pour out as much of the liquid as possible. Be liberal with the grated nutmeg and add a little salt. Then stir in the cream little by little, getting the spinach to absorb as much as possible. Keep warm.

Remove the bacon and slice it fairly thickly. Arrange it on a serving platter on top of the creamed spinach. Keep warm. Strain the pan juices and boil vigorously for a moment or two. Thicken with arrowroot if desired and then add the rest of the Madeira. Pour over the meat and serve.

SERVES 4 to 6.

Cider Ham

1 ham – size depending on how many you want to
   serve
6 peppercorns
enough cider
2 teacups moist brown sugar
1 tablespoon mustard *or* to taste

Soak the ham overnight if it is salt.

Drain it and put it in a large pan with the pepper and enough dry cider to cover it. Bring slowly to the boil and then simmer it for 15 minutes to the pound and 15 minutes over. Keep skimming. Remove the ham.

Cut off the rind and place the ham in a baking dish. Mix the sugar and mustard with enough cider stock to make a stiffish paste. Spread it over the meat. Cook it at the top of a very hot oven for a very few minutes until the sugar bubbles and becomes crisp. Then move it to the bottom of the oven for about another 30 minutes. Should the sugar start to burn, turn the heat down a little. Eat hot or cold.

SERVES as many as the size of the ham dictates.

Don't throw the rest of the stock away. Use it instead of water to make up almost any packet soup, especially a ham one.

Ham in Asparagus Sauce

An ideal dish to put in an automatic oven, to be cooked by the time you get home.

25 g (1 oz) butter *or* less
1 chopped onion
1 tin Campbell's condensed cream of chicken soup
2 tablespoons sherry
225 g (8 oz) cooked ham
1 tin asparagus tips, drained
75 g (3 oz) grated hard cheese

Melt the butter and sauté the onion until transparent. Then stir in the soup and sherry. Put the diced ham in a small ovenproof casserole, with the asparagus on top. Pour the soup over and sprinkle with the cheese. Bake in a fairly hot oven for 30 minutes. Serve with rice or creamed potatoes.

SERVES 4.

Ham Steaks with a Mushroom and Wine Sauce

Make this simple recipe with Marks and Spencer ham steaks; much more exciting than merely grilled and not much more trouble.

25 g (1 oz) butter
4 ham steaks (*or* bacon steaks)
25 g (1 oz) flour
275 ml (½ pint) white wine
125 g (4 oz) mushrooms
1 small carton double cream

Melt the butter, fry the steaks until golden brown on both sides. Remove the steaks from the pan and keep warm in a serving dish. Stir in the flour and cook for 1 minute, then add the wine and boil vigorously until reduced by about a third. Stir in the sliced mushrooms and simmer for 2 to 3 minutes. Stir the cream into the sauce and warm through. Pour over the steaks and serve immediately.

SERVES 4.

This recipe can be used for turkey breasts, only you need a little more butter in which to fry them.

Dream Ham

A very good quick supper dish which is easy to prepare and it tastes good too.

12 slices cooked ham, soaked in sherry
225 g (8 oz) mushrooms
butter
1 tin pimentos, drained
grated cheese
275 ml (½ pint) double cream
2–3 dessertspoons chilli sauce

Roll the slices of ham and lay them in the bottom of a buttered ovenproof dish. Fry the mushrooms lightly and lay them on top of the ham. Thinly slice the pimentos and roll them in plenty of cheese, and place on top of the mushrooms. Whip the cream lightly, add the chilli sauce and pour over the ham. Cook in a moderately warm oven for about 25 minutes.

Rice and salad go very well.

SERVES 6.

Orange Ham Rolls

A very simple supper dish. More interesting than sliced cold ham.

a few raisins
2 tablespoons orange liqueur
1 large carton cottage cheese
2 peeled and diced oranges
6 slices cooked ham

Leave the raisins to soak in the liqueur for about 30

minutes and then mix together with the cottage cheese and orange. Divide the mixture on to the middle of each ham slice and roll up the ham. Serve with a green salad.

SERVES 3.

Lamb Cutlets with Reform Sauce

This is richer and better than plain grilled cutlets. It's not much effort except that you have to wash two more pans.

8 lamb cutlets *or* 4 large chump chops
seasoned flour
1 beaten egg
breadcrumbs
50 g (2 oz) butter
1 rasher streaky bacon
1 small onion
1 carrot
50 g (2 oz) flour
1 skinned tomato
550 ml (1 pint) stock (made from cube)
1 bouquet garni
pepper and salt
1 tablespoon redcurrant *or* apple jelly
1 tablespoon port

Remove the fat from the cutlets. Dip each one in seasoned flour, egg and then breadcrumbs. Keep covered until needed.

Melt the butter, remove the rind from the bacon, chop into small pieces, fry with the chopped onion and chopped carrot. When they are brown, work in the flour and continue cooking for a few minutes. Then stir in the chopped tomato and gradually add the stock, bouquet garni and seasoning. Cover and simmer for about 45 minutes, by which time the liquid should have reduced considerably. If there is need, skim the sauce and strain into a clean pan. Stir in the jelly and port and warm through until the jelly melts.

In a separate pan fry the cutlets until cooked. (Ideally use deep fat and drain on kitchen paper.) Serve the sauce separately.

SERVES 4.

Lamb with Sour Cream

If your butcher provides boned rolled shoulders of lamb this makes a good dinner party dish quite cheaply.

a little oil *or* butter
1 boned rolled shoulder of lamb
2 onions
2 carrots
2 sticks of celery
2 bay leaves
pinch of thyme
190 ml ($\frac{1}{3}$ pint) red wine
3 dessertspoons redcurrant *or* apple jelly
1 carton sour cream

Heat the butter or oil in a casserole and quickly brown the meat all over. Remove the meat and add the chopped vegetables. Gently fry them until they start to turn brown. Remove the casserole from the heat, replace the meat, add the bay leaves and thyme and pour in the wine. Stew in a moderate oven allowing 30 minutes per pound weight of the lamb. When the lamb is cooked put it on a carving dish and keep warm. Strain the wine juices into a separate pan and boil for 5 minutes. Stir in the jelly and cream and allow to warm through. Serve the sauce separately.

SERVES 6 using a whole shoulder.

Lamb Bourgignon

Better-quality lamb is often the same price as stewing beef which means it needs less time to cook and so is cheaper.

1 tablespoon olive oil
125 g (4 oz) bacon
1 onion
1 clove garlic
675 g (1 lb 8 oz) good-quality stewing lamb
a little flour
1 carrot
1 tablespoon tomato purée
425 ml (¾ pint) red wine
a little sugar
salt and pepper
125 g (4 oz) mushrooms

Heat the oil and fry the chopped bacon until cooked. Remove with a slotted spoon and fry the chopped onion and crushed garlic. Remove all fat from the lamb and cut into bite-size cubes. Sprinkle with flour and add the vegetables with the chopped carrots. Fry, turning often, until the meat is brown. Add the cooked bacon. Then stir in the tomato purée, pour on the wine and season with a little sugar, salt and pepper. Bring to the boil and cook in a moderate oven for 1 hour 30 minutes. Thirty minutes before serving, add the mushrooms, chopped if large, whole if button. (You can, if you want to leave the casserole unattended for the cooking time, put the mushrooms in at the start, but I like them not to get soggy, so put mine in later.)

SERVES 4.

Lamb Chops with Provençale Sauce

In this case, the sauce is mostly chopped tomatoes and constitutes a second vegetable.

4 lamb chops *or* 8 noisettes if you can get them
cooking oil if necessary
3 tablespoons olive oil
1 large onion
2 cloves garlic (or less)
450 g (1 lb) tomatoes

1 tablespoon tomato purée
salt and pepper
few sprigs chopped parsley
150 ml (¼ pint) dry white wine

Grill the chops or fry the noisettes.

Make the sauce by heating oil and gently frying the chopped onion and crushed garlic. Do not allow to brown. Meanwhile skin the tomatoes (by dipping in boiling water) and chop them into fairly small pieces. Do this in a bowl so as not to lose the tomato juice. Add them, with the tomato purée, seasonings and wine to the pan. Bring to the boil and cook over none too low a heat for about 10 minutes. Arrange the chops in the middle of a serving dish surrounded by the tomatoes. Sprinkle with parsley.

SERVES 4.

Lamb Chops with Gooseberry Sauce

This sauce makes a change from the endless redcurrant jelly alternating with mint sauce. It tastes good too.

8 small lamb cutlets *or* 4 large chops
2 tablespoons cider *or* Cinzano
25 g (1 oz) butter
450 g (1 lb) gooseberries
seasoning
1 tablespoon sugar
nutmeg if liked

Trim off as much fat as possible from the chops. Place under a hot grill for a couple of minutes each side, then turn down heat and cook gently until cooked through.

Meanwhile heat the cider and butter and add the washed gooseberries. When soft and mushy, liquidize and sieve. Season. Then add the sugar and nutmeg to taste – don't make the sauce too sweet. Serve either hot or cold.

It'll keep in an airtight jar in the fridge for several days, so you could save time and make extra quantities during the gooseberry season. This can also be made by draining the liquid off tinned gooseberries, heating them with a little cider or Cinzano and then sieving them, but don't add any sugar.

SERVES 4.

Lamb Shaslik

No sheep's eyes in this – suitable for the most refined Western palate.

> 450 g (1 lb) lamb (from the leg *or* shoulder)
> 1 small onion
> lemon juice
> 2 tablespoons wine
> seasoning
> 6 to 8 small tomatoes
> 6 to 8 small mushrooms

Trim the fat from the meat and cut the meat into small cubes. Marinate the meat overnight with sliced onion, lemon juice, wine and seasoning. Put the meat on skewers, alternating the tomatoes and mushrooms. Grill. Serve on the skewers on a bed of savoury rice.

SERVES 3.

Devilled Kidneys

> 18 lambs' kidneys
> 12 dried prunes
> seasoned flour
> 125 g (4 oz) butter
> 1 miniature bottle apricot brandy
> 550 ml (1 pint) meat stock
> seasoning

Trim the kidneys, removing the white core and outer skin.

Cut into pieces. Stone the prunes (there is no need to soak them). Roll the kidneys in the seasoned flour and sauté in half the butter for about 7 minutes. Pour over the apricot brandy and flame. Add the stock and simmer for about 10 minutes. Whilst the kidneys are simmering, sauté the prunes in the rest of the butter separately until they are just tender – about 7 minutes. Transfer both the prunes and the kidneys to a casserole dish together with the liquid and season well. Cook for about 15 minutes in a moderate oven. As this dish is quite sweet, I suggest you serve it with rice and a plain green salad.

SERVES 6.

Liver with Mustard and Cointreau

A most successful way of making liver absolutely scrummy – it is very important, however, that the liver is not over-cooked and it should be served immediately.

    4 slices of liver
    seasoned flour
    2 tablespoons oil
    2 tablespoons French mustard
    1 tablespoon finely chopped onion *or* shallot
    2 tablespoons finely chopped parsley
    1 tablespoon Cointreau
    fresh white breadcrumbs
    50 g (2 oz) melted butter
    orange slices and watercress to garnish

Roll the liver slices in seasoned flour and fry in the hot oil for about 1 minute each side. Remove. Mix the mustard, onion and parsley, and add enough Cointreau to make it a creamy mixture. Spread the mixture on to the liver slices and coat with breadcrumbs, press these on firmly. Put the slices under the grill coated with half the butter and leave for a couple of minutes, and then turn them and re-coat them with the remaining butter – until brown on both sides.

Place a thin orange slice on top of each piece under the grill for a few seconds and then garnish with watercress before serving.

SERVES 4.

Lemon Liver

This is my favourite way of cooking liver as the combination of lemon and wine removes all the livery taste. Delicious and takes no time at all to prepare.

  1 tablespoon oil
  450 g (1 lb) liver
  1 heaped tablespoon flour
  150 ml ($\frac{1}{4}$ pint) white wine
  125 g (4 oz) mushrooms
  rind and juice of $\frac{1}{2}$ lemon
  bay leaf
  thyme
  salt and pepper
  4 rashers bacon, not too fatty

Heat the oil and fry the diced liver until sealed. Stir in the flour and cook for a moment or two longer. Gradually add the wine and then all the other ingredients except the bacon. Bring to the boil and then cook in a slow oven for 1 hour. Just before serving, fry the bacon, cut up into small pieces, until cooked but not crisp. Add to the casserole, remove bay leaf and serve.

SERVES 4.

Pork Chops with Winey Prunes

Excellent.

  12 prunes
  $\frac{1}{4}$ bottle white wine

4 large pork chops *or* pork fillets
seasoned flour
25 g (1 oz) butter
1 tablespoon oil
1 tablespoon redcurrant jelly
½ small carton double cream

Simmer the prunes in half the wine for about 30 minutes.
Keep warm. Flatten the chops, bone them if you wish and
coat in seasoned flour. Melt the butter with the oil, fry the
chops until brown on each side (about 5 minutes). Then
add the rest of the wine, cover and simmer until the meat is
cooked; this should take a further 20 minutes. Remove the
meat and arrange on a serving dish with the prunes. Keep
warm. Add the wine from the prunes to the pan and boil
until reduced by half. Then stir in the redcurrant jelly and
the cream. Boil until the sauce thickens, when you pour it
over the meat and prunes. Serve.

SERVES 4.

Roast Pork with Orange Sauce

Makes an interesting change from apple sauce.

1 2¼ kg (5 lb) roast of pork
1 *or* 2 cloves garlic
a little chopped parsley
marjoram
rosemary
salt and freshly milled black pepper
1 tablespoon oil
275 ml (½ pint) chicken stock
3 oranges
150 ml (¼ pint) white wine

Remove most of the fat from the pork. Mix together the
garlic, parsley, marjoram, rosemary, salt and pepper and
rub this mixture into the joint. Heat the oil in a baking tin
and add the pork. Roast in a fairly hot oven for about 15

minutes. Pour over the chicken stock and roast in a very slow oven for almost 3 hours, basting from time to time. During the last 15 minutes of the roasting, add the juice of 1 orange and the wine.

Finely slice the other 2 oranges and blanch briefly in boiling water. Spread them round the joint for the last few minutes of roasting time.

To serve, decorate the pork with the sliced oranges and hand the sauce round separately. If the meat has oozed too much fat, skim it off before serving.

SERVES 6 to 8.

Pork Chops with Piquant Sauce

This is remarkably good and easy; if made the evening before it heats up happily.

    4 pork chops
    25 g (1 oz) butter
    4 onions
    salt and pepper
    1 tablespoon flour
    190 ml (about ⅓ pint) water
    1 teaspoon vinegar
    1 tablespoon sharp sauce, i.e. pickle *or* sliced gherkins
    2 tablespoons Madeira

Remove all excess fat from the chops. Heat the butter and brown the chops on both sides. Add the peeled and sliced onions and continue to cook until they are transparent. Remove the chops to a warm place. Season. Stir in the flour and keep cooking until it browns. Then work in the water, vinegar and pickles. Cook gently for 5 minutes. Taste. It should be sharp, if not add a little more pickles or whatever you have of that ilk in your cupboard. Then return the chops and either simmer for a further 15 minutes or cook in a moderate oven for a similar period. Just before serving stir in the Madeira.

SERVES 4.

Chops with Creamed Carrots

This is easy, takes very little time to prepare and can in fact be prepared the day before. Just heat it when needed.

    4 pork chops (*or* lamb chops if preferred)
    125 g (4 oz) butter
    2 425 g (15 oz) tins carrots *or* about 900 g (2 lb) cooked
        carrots
    salt and pepper
    2 tablespoons sweet sherry *or* Madeira
    2½ tablespoons double cream plus another tablespoon

Trim all excess fat off chops. Melt the butter and fry the chops gently until they are brown on both sides.

Drain the warmed carrots really thoroughly. Mash them with a fork with salt and pepper. Heat the sherry and cream to boiling point and then beat into the mashed carrot.

Pile the carrots into the centre of an ovenproof dish, making an indentation on the top with the back of a spoon, pour the last tablespoon of cream into this. Arrange the chops around the carrots and cover. Bake in a medium oven for 30 minutes.

SERVES 4.

Chops Baked with Nuts and Vegetables

If you want to prepare this foolproof dish in advance, work through the recipe until the cooking-in-the-oven stage. It can happily be made the night before and heated for an hour when needed.

    25 g (1 oz) butter
    4 pork chops
    2 small onions
    4 sticks celery
    4 dessertspoons salted peanuts
    1 medium tin tomatoes
    seasoning
    ½ bottle white wine

Melt the butter and gently fry the chops until they are golden on both sides.

Peel and slice the onions as finely as you can. Scrape and chop the celery equally fine. Mix the onion, celery and nuts into the tomatoes, trying to break them down as well.

Put half the mixture into a casserole, place the chops on top, add the rest of the mixture. Season well and pour the wine over the lot.

Put the lid on the casserole and bake in a medium oven for about 1 hour.

SERVES 4.

Pork Chops with Winey Cabbage

> 1 small white cabbage
> 1 small carton single cream *or* yoghurt
> salt and pepper
> 4 pork chops
> 25 g (1 oz) butter
> 150 ml ($\frac{1}{4}$ pint) white wine
> pinch of caraway
> grated Parmesan
> dabs of butter

Slice the cabbage finely and boil in salted water for 5 minutes. Drain and return to pan with the cream, salt and pepper. Simmer for 30 minutes. Meanwhile trim excess fat off the chops. Melt the butter and fry chops until golden on both sides. Remove the chops from the pan, add the wine and caraway and cook for a couple of minutes. When the cabbage is cooked add the wine juices. Put half the cabbage in a casserole, lay the chops on top and spread with the remaining cabbage. Sprinkle with grated Parmesan and dot with butter. Bake for 30 minutes in a medium oven.

SERVES 4.

Pork Marengo

This is not complicated, can be prepared in advance and should be served with rice.

575 g (1 lb 4 oz) boneless pork chops *or* fillet
1 tablespoon olive oil
2 medium onions
1 tablespoon flour
150 ml (¼ pint) white wine
225 g (8 oz) tin tomatoes
bay leaf
salt and pepper
1 teaspoon sugar

Remove the fat from the chops and cut into cubes. Heat the olive oil in a flameproof pan and gently fry the meat until it is golden all over. Peel and chop the onions. Remove the meat from the pan, add the onions and fry until they are transparent. Work in the flour and after a minute add the wine. When this is hot, add the tomatoes, bay leaf, salt, pepper and sugar. Bring to the boil, stirring all the time. Then put the meat back into the pan, cover and cook in a slow oven for 1 hour.

SERVES 4.

Pork Chops with Sultanas

Another dish which can be prepared in advance.

4 pork chops
50 g (2 oz) butter
1 dessertspoon flour
juice and grated rind of 1 lemon
275 ml (½ pint) sherry, Madeira *or* cider
50 g (2 oz) sultanas
2 peeled, cored and sliced apples
salt, pepper and nutmeg

Remove excess fat from the chops. Heat the butter in a pan

and gently fry the chops until golden brown. Put them into a casserole. Meanwhile stir the flour into the remaining butter in the pan. When this has been worked in and taken up all the bits, add the lemon and liquor. Cook until boiling then add the fruit and seasoning. Pour the sauce over the chops and bake in a medium oven for 1 hour.

SERVES 4.

Hungarian Pork Fillet

This is not extravagant – although many people are under the false impression that it is – and the meat is so tender.

> 1 small onion
> 25 g (1 oz) butter
> 2 pork fillets (about 225–350 g (8–12 oz) each) *or* boneless chops, diced
> seasoning
> juice of ½ lemon
> 1 glass white wine *or* sherry
> 1 dessertspoon flour
> 125 g (4 oz) sliced mushrooms
> 150 ml (¼ pint) good chicken stock *or* 1 tin consommé
> 1 carton sour cream *or* yoghurt
> paprika

Chop the onion finely. Place in a sauté or deep frying pan with the butter, and cook slowly until just colouring. Put in the fillets, increase the heat slightly and brown on all sides. Season, add the lemon juice and wine, cover the pan and cook for 15 minutes. Take out the pork, skim off the butter and mix with the flour. Return to the pan and stir until boiling. Add the mushrooms and the stock and simmer 5 minutes. Meantime slice the fillets of pork and return them to the pan with the sour cream and sprinkle with paprika. Heat carefully and then serve with vegetables.

SERVES 6.

Pork Chops with Orange Sauce

This has a light and refreshing flavour.

4 pork chops
1 tablespoon oil
½ orange
1 onion
2 stalks celery
1 *or* 2 crushed cloves garlic
1 glass orange juice
1 teaspoon vinegar
 a pinch of thyme
salt and pepper
3 tablespoons orange liqueur

Brown the chops on both sides. Arrange them in a lidded fireproof dish with a half-slice of orange on each. Chop the vegetables finely, brown them in the frying pan and spread them on the chops. Mix the orange juice, vinegar, thyme, salt and pepper together and add about 3 tablespoons orange liqueur. Pour over the chops and cook in a moderate oven for about 45 minutes. Remove the lid and brown for another 15 minutes.

SERVES 4.

Pork or Lamb Chops made more Interesting

The only excitement in this is a delicious sauce that can be made practically in the time it takes the chops to grill.

25 g (1 oz) butter
1 medium onion
1 crushed clove garlic
25 g (1 oz) flour
1 tin tomatoes
1 glass red wine
ground black pepper

Melt the butter, add the chopped onion and garlic. Cook till soft. Add the flour, cook for 1 minute then add the tomatoes. Stir until they are broken up, then add the wine and cook a little longer. Make it as garlicky and peppery as you like.

You can put the cooked chops in a bowl and pour the sauce over or you can serve the sauce separately. The sauce keeps well so it is worth making a double quantity.

SERVES 4.

Pernod Pork in Breadcrumbs

Just the thing for the jaded palate – you'll like it.

> 4 loin pork chops
> 1 beaten egg
> seasoned breadcrumbs
> 2 tablespoons cooking oil
> 1 tablespoon flour
> 2 wineglasses tomato juice
> 150 ml (about ¼ pint) stock
> 2 tablespoons Pernod
> seasoning

Remove the bones from the chops and hammer meat well until flattened. Dip in the egg mixture and coat with seasoned breadcrumbs. Fry the chops in the oil until brown. Keep warm. Make the sauce by adding flour to the juices together with the tomato juice and some stock. Reduce, stirring all the time. If it gets too thick add more stock. Just before serving add the liquor, season well and pour over the chops.

SERVES 4.

Pernod Pork

This is a more simplified edition of the previous recipe.

6 pork chops
seasoning
3 tablespoons Pernod
2 tablespoons oil
2 cloves garlic
150 ml (¼ pint) stock

Marinate the chops, well seasoned, in half the Pernod for about 12 hours. Warm the oil with the crushed garlic and fry the chops until brown. Heat the stock with the rest of the Pernod. Pour any excess fat off the chops and add the stock. Cover and simmer for about 25 minutes, without burning the chops.

SERVES 6.

Pork Chops Savoy

This dish can easily be prepared a day in advance and re-heated.

50 g (2 oz) butter
4 pork chops
1 dessertspoon flour
150 ml (¼ pint) sherry
1 lemon
25 g (1 oz) sultanas
1 apple

Melt the butter in a pan and brown the chops on all sides. Put the chops in a fireproof dish. Add the flour to the fat in the pan and stir until brown. Stir in the sherry and the juice and grated rind of the lemon. When smooth add the sultanas and the apple, peeled, cored and diced. Season the sauce and pour it over the chops. Cook in a moderate oven for almost 1 hour.

SERVES 4.

Pot-roasted Veal with Orange and Mustard Sauce

This is a good dinner-party dish and not particularly tiresome to do. As the meat is cooked in soup do not add salt, there'll be plenty.

>   1 tablespoon olive oil
>   1 1⅓ kg (3 lb) roast of veal
>   2 old carrots
>   1 tin concentrated onion soup
>   50 g (2 oz) almonds
>   salt
>   25 g (1 oz) butter
>   25 g (1 oz) flour
>   1 teaspoon mild mustard (or more)
>   rind and juice of 1 orange
>   2 tablespoons Cointreau, Grand Marnier *or* Curaçao
>   ½ small carton double cream

Heat the oil in an ovenproof casserole, then fry the meat until it is brown all over. Add the carrots, roughly chopped, and the soup, together with half a tinful of water. Cover and roast for 2 hours in a hot oven, basting occasionally. At the same time bake the almonds in a fireproof dish with a little olive oil and some salt. Cook till brown (about 30 minutes). I always cook double quantities as I so like salted almonds.

When the meat is cooked, take it out and carve it fairly thickly. Cover with foil and keep warm. Reduce the roast stock to nearly half by boiling vigorously. In another pan melt the butter, stir in the flour and gradually add the strained stock. Then add the mustard, orange juice and finely chopped rind, together with the liqueur. Taste it, I like double quantities of mustard but see if there is enough to your taste at this stage; if not add more. Stir in the cream. Sprinkle the nuts over the meat and pour the sauce over the lot. This will happily keep warm in a low oven for some time, but it must be covered.

SERVES 6.

Roman Veal

>   4 veal steaks
>   2 crushed cloves garlic
>   salt and pepper
>   sage
>   4 slices smoked ham
>   25 g (1 oz) butter
>   2 glasses white wine
>   ½ small carton double cream

Pound the veal to make it as thin as possible. Rub it over with the garlic and seasoning and sprinkle each steak with a pinch of sage. Fasten a piece of ham on each steak with a toothpick. Melt the butter and fry the meat until brown. Pour the first glass of wine over the meat. Remove the meat and keep hot. Pour in the second glass of wine and scrape up bits in pan. Stir in the cream, heat through, pour over the meat and serve at once.

SERVES 4.

Quick and Easy Veal

>   2 large onions
>   4 fillets of veal
>   225 g (8 oz) grated Cheddar cheese
>   white wine
>   seasoning
>   flour

Chop the onions and lay them in the bottom of a fireproof dish. Put a layer of veal on top, and then a layer of grated cheese on top of the veal. Add enough wine to cover the veal, season and cook in a moderate oven for about 1 hour. Thicken with flour just before serving.

SERVES 4.

Chilled Veal with Artichokes

> 6 Jerusalem artichokes
> 125 g (4 oz) butter
> 2 tablespoons flour
> 550 ml (1 pint) milk
> 125 g (4 oz) grated mild cheese
> 5 tablespoons sherry
> seasoning
> 6 fillets of veal
> 1 tin mixed peppers, tomatoes and aubergines

Peel and slice the artichokes. Boil them in salted water for about 15 minutes. Make a white sauce with half the butter, flour and milk. Boil for about 2 minutes. Remove from the heat and add the cheese, sherry and seasoning. Cover the pan and leave to cool. Melt the rest of the butter and sauté the veal for 1 minute on each side. Remove from the pan. Mash together the artichokes, peppers, tomatoes and aubergines. Cover the fillets with the mixture, roll them up and fix with two cocktail sticks. Place them in a serving dish (sticks facing upwards) pour the sauce over and chill until needed.

SERVES 6.

Veal with Cream Cheese

This recipe is fairly rich so don't have a heavy starter beforehand.

> 8 escalopes
> 4 slices Parma ham
> 1 packet cream cheese
> 2 tablespoons grated Parmesan
> 1 tablespoon finely chopped chives
> seasoning
> 3 tablespoons double cream
> flour
> butter
> 150 ml ($\frac{1}{4}$ pint) white wine

Hammer the escalopes until thin. Place a ham slice on four of the escalopes. Mix the cream cheese, Parmesan, chives and seasoning with enough cream to soften. Spread this mixture on top of the ham and then cover with the remaining four escalopes. Beat the edges so as to join firmly. Dip the escalopes in flour, melt the butter and brown the escalopes on both sides. Add the wine and seasoning and simmer for about 20 minutes.

SERVES 4.

French Roast Veal

This recipe takes a little more effort than most but is well worth it for an occasion.

> 75 g (3 oz) butter
> 1⅓–1¾ kg (3–4 lb) veal roast
> 1 sliced carrot
> 1 sliced medium onion
> 275 ml (½ pint) white wine
> bouquet garni
> several bacon rinds
> salt and pepper
> *for garniture:*
> 25 g (1 oz) butter
> 3 rashers chopped lean bacon
> 12 small shallots *or* 3 small chopped onions
> 6 sliced baby carrots
> 190 ml (⅓ pint) consommé
> salt and pepper
> 1 tablespoon sugar

Melt the butter in a large flameproof casserole. Brown the piece of veal all over. Add the vegetables, wine, bouquet garni, bacon rinds and seasoning. Cover the casserole and bake in a moderate oven for 1½ hours, then uncover and bake for a further 30 minutes. Remove the bouquet garni and bacon rinds. Slice the roast on to a serving dish, pour the sauce over and surround it with the following garniture.

Melt the butter and fry the bacon in it. Then add the onions, and fry until transparent, at which stage add the carrots. Fry until the carrots get brown, then pour on the consommé, sugar and seasoning. Cover and simmer until the majority of the liquid is absorbed (about 30 minutes).

SERVES 6 to 8.

Veal Stew

Put this on at tea time and forget it till dinner time. Simplicity.

> 675 g (1 lb 8 oz) veal
> 25 g (1 oz) butter
> 25 g (1 oz) flour
> ½ bottle red wine *or* more if necessary
> seasoning
> 1 *or* 2 cloves garlic, crushed
> chopped parsley
> 1 bay leaf

Cut the veal into 2½-cm (1-inch) cubes. Melt the butter in a casserole and sauté the veal until lightly browned. Work the flour into the meat and fat. Add the rest of the ingredients, cover and simmer for about 2½ hours, being careful not to let the liquid reduce too much. Add more wine if necessary.

SERVES 4.

Paupiettes de Veau

This is a delicious way of serving veal and somewhat different from the more conventional veal sauces. It can easily be prepared in advance but should not be cooked until wanted.

> 8 veal escalopes

stuffing:

    125 g (4 oz) sausage meat
    ½ cup crumbled stale bread soaked in hot milk and
        squeezed dry
    1 beaten egg
    1 tablespoon minced parsley
    a little black pepper
    2 tablespoons butter
    ½ cup white wine
    a little stock
    ¼ cup single cream

Pound the escalopes until thin and trim. Mix the stuffing
and add the scraps from the escalopes to it. Spread the
stuffing on the escalopes and roll them up neatly and tie
with kitchen thread.

Melt the butter and add the veal birds and simmer them
turning several times for 30 minutes, being careful not to
brown them. Add the wine and braise the veal for about 1
hour until it is cooked and tender.

Transfer the veal to a heated dish and cut off the threads.
Add a little hot stock and cream to the pan and reduce over
a hot flame for 2 or 3 minutes. Pour the sauce over the
veal.

This dish is excellent served with sautéed whole mushrooms or alternatively add 125 g (4 oz) chopped mushrooms
to the pan before adding the cream.

SERVES 8.

Wiener Schnitzel with Whisky Sauce

Which makes an interesting change.

    4 veal fillets
    beaten egg and breadcrumbs to coat
    50 g (2 oz) butter
    275 ml (just under ½ pint) of thick white sauce
    150 ml (1 gill) whisky
    1 small tin tomato paste

    1 bay leaf
    thyme
    1 finely chopped stick celery
    1 finely chopped small onion
    salt and pepper
    sliced stuffed green olives
    a few anchovy fillets for garnish

Dip the veal fillets in egg and breadcrumbs. Heat the butter and fry the veal gently until golden brown. To the white sauce, add the whisky, tomato paste, bay leaf, thyme, celery, onion, salt and pepper. Cook for several minutes and remove the bay leaf. Arrange veal on serving dish, pour the sauce over and decorate with olives and anchovies. Serve at once.

SERVES 4.

Escalopes with Oranges

This I really like.

    50 g (2 oz) butter
    4 veal escalopes
    25 g (1 oz) flour
    2 oranges
    4 tablespoons orange liqueur
    75 ml ($\frac{1}{8}$ pint) chicken stock
    seasoning
    parsley to garnish

Melt the butter in a large pan and sauté the escalopes until slightly brown on both sides. Take out the escalopes, remove the pan from the heat and stir in the flour. Add the rind and juice of 1 orange, the liqueur and the stock. Reheat, replace the veal and season well, cover and simmer for about 10 minutes. Pour into a serving dish and garnish with parsley and the remaining orange finely sliced.

SERVES 4.

Veal in Vermouth

Even a bedsit-bound cook can manage this triumph.

6 veal escalopes
seasoning
flour
3 tablespoons butter
225 g (8 oz) button mushrooms
3 tablespoons dry Vermouth
1 small carton double cream
cayenne pepper

Hammer the escalopes until fairly thin. Season well and coat in flour. Melt the butter and fry the meat on both sides until cooked and tender (do not overcook). Remove and keep warm. Cook the mushrooms in the pan for about 5 minutes, add the Vermouth, cream and seasoning. When hot but not boiling, pour over the veal and serve.

SERVES 6.

Kidney Veal Chops

Veal chops are not cheap so they deserve a little more effort in preparation. It's worth it.

40 g (1½ oz) butter
4 veal chops with kidneys
225 g (8 oz) washed button mushrooms
a little chicken stock
1 dessertspoon arrowroot *or* cornflour
a small carton single cream
1 sherry-glass sherry
salt and pepper

Melt the butter and quickly brown the chops on both sides. Cover and simmer for about 20 minutes, turning them and adding more butter if necessary. Add most of the mushrooms and toss them in the butter for about 5 minutes. Remove the meat and mushrooms and keep warm. Add the stock to the pan, and scrape well in order to remove the goodness from the bottom of the pan. Mix the arrowroot with a little water and add to the stock, together with the cream and sherry. Season. Heat the sauce but do not allow it to boil. Pour over the chops and mushrooms before serving and garnish with the few remaining mushrooms.

SERVES 4.

Elegant Veal Chops

Try this for a delicious dinner à deux.

>   50 g (2 oz) butter
>   1 onion
>   2 rashers lean bacon
>   25 g (1 oz) butter
>   2 veal chops
>   75 ml ($\frac{1}{8}$ pint) light stock
>   1 glass wine
>   salt and pepper
>   1 egg yolk
>   a little chopped parsley

Melt the butter and sauté the chopped onion and diced bacon until golden brown. Add more butter and the chops and cook slowly until brown, turning occasionally. Remove chops when they are cooked and keep warm. Pour away a little of the fat from the pan and add the stock and the wine. Simmer and season with salt and pepper. Beat the egg yolk. Remove the stock from the heat and gradually add to the egg yolk, stirring constantly. Reheat the sauce and add the parsley. Take care not to let it boil. Pour over the chops just before serving.

SERVES 2.

My Grandma Mathieson's Grandma Ockleston's Jugged Hare

Which is excellent but rather costly – port was cheaper in those days. But you can easily substitute wine for port. Haig, the whisky people, recommend you substitute whisky in any jugged hare recipe, but superb though it sounds I've never felt rich enough to try – perhaps when I've a good supply of duty-free!

    2 onions
    marjoram
    6 cloves
    1 blade of mace
    nutmeg
    peppercorns
    bay leaves
    juniper berries
    2 tablespoons oil
    550 ml (1 pint) port
    1 washed jointed hare
    oil
    2 more onions
    more port
    a little stock *or* milk
    2 tablespoons redcurrant *or* apple jelly
    cornflour

Add all the preceding ingredients to the port and pour them over the hare. Let it stand in the marinade overnight. (In my great-great-grandmother's day they left it in the coolest part of the oven for a shorter time, but overnight in a colder place is more convenient nowadays.) Heat the second oil, finely chop the onions and fry them until they are transparent. Then remove the hare from the marinade, dry the pieces and fry them in the oil until they are brown. Pour in the marinade and more port (probably another glass) and either a little stock or milk. Bring to the boil. Transfer to a heavy casserole and bake in a low oven for 2 hours or more.

Remove the hare pieces and keep them warm. Strain the

sauce into a clean pan and stir in the redcurrant or apple jelly, though my great-great-granny used blackcurrant. Thicken the sauce with a little cornflour and if you have any of the blood stir that in. Keep stirring and cook, without boiling, for several minutes. Then pour it over the meat and serve with rice.

SERVES 6 or more depending on the size of the hare.

Duck with Apple

This saves the effort of making apple sauce but looks as if you went to infinitely more trouble.

> 1 duck
> apples
> lemon juice
> 1 glass Calvados
> salt and pepper

Roast the duck in the usual way but stuff it with peeled and roughly chopped apples. Just before serving peel and finely slice a few more good eating apples. Put the duck on to a carving dish, surround it with the sliced apples (sprinkled with lemon juice to keep their colour) and pour the Calvados over the bird. Light it, carve and eat.

SERVES 3 or more depending on the size of the bird.

Duck with Orange Sauce

Duck is a greasy bird so is always served with a sharp accompaniment to offset the fattiness. When cooking a duck, keep pricking it to release as much of the fat as possible; if need be cook it longer than traditionalists would advise.

If you haven't the time to make this extremely simple sauce, you should at least cut an orange in two and stuff it into the duck before cooking it. Then serve the duck with cold sliced oranges sprinkled with Cointreau.

1 duck of a size to serve your guests (it doesn't go very far)
2 oranges
1 lemon
1 tablespoon sugar
2 tablespoons vinegar
2 peeled oranges, sliced (optional for garnish)
2 tablespoons brandy *or* an orange liqueur
¼ cup consommé *or* chicken stock

Roast the duck in a hot oven for about 1 hour. Keep pricking and basting it.

Peel the two oranges and the lemon. Squeeze them and remove the pith from the peel and finely chop the peel. Pour boiling water over it and leave for a few seconds. Strain. Dissolve the sugar in the vinegar and heat until it caramelizes. Then add the juice of the oranges and lemon and the peels. Cook gently. When the duck is done, arrange on a carving dish with the sliced oranges if wanted. Pour all fat off the roasting pan and stir in liquor and consommé. Stir vigorously and get all the bits off the pan. Then add the orange sauce, heat through and serve. It's excellent.

The sauce is enough for 4.

Boozy Pheasant

A glorious dish.

a generous wineglass brandy } *or* 2 glasses
ditto of port   } sweet sherry
1 pheasant
75 g (3 oz) butter
50 g (2 oz) peeled almonds
salt and pepper
cornflour

Pour the liquor over the bird and leave it to soak in the marinade at least overnight. Either cover or turn it now and then, or both. Melt the butter in a casserole and fry the almonds (add a dash of oil to prevent the butter from burning). Remove the nuts and cook the bird, until it is brown all over. Replace the nuts, pour in the liquor and season. Cover and cook in a medium oven for about 1 hour (time depending on size of bird). When it is cooked remove the bird and keep warm.

Stir a little cornflour into the pan juices and bring to the boil. Add a little more liquor or stock if there is not enough liquid.

SERVES 2 or 3; it is rarely possible to get a pheasant to feed more.

Pheasant with Apples and Cream

If you are lucky enough ever to get to the stage of being bored with roast pheasant, breadcrumbs and potato crisps, this makes an original and very easy alternative.

25 g (1 oz) butter
1 tablespoon oil
1 large chopped onion
1 pheasant
3 tablespoons Calvados *or* brandy
425 ml ($\frac{3}{4}$ pint) chicken stock
150 ml ($\frac{1}{4}$ pint) double cream
225 g (8 oz) peeled and sliced eating apples
salt and pepper
2 large apples cored and sliced into rings, fried in butter

Heat the butter and oil and fry the onion until it is transparent. Remove it and fry the pheasant until it is brown. Do this gently. Replace the onion, remove excess fat if any. Warm the liqueur in a ladle, set fire to it and pour it over the bird. Then add the stock, cream, apples and seasoning. Cover and bake in a medium oven for about 1 hour. Perfectionists carve the bird, arrange it on a dish, strain the sauce and pour it over the bird. The rest serve the sauce separately. Both decorate the serving dish with apple rings fried in butter.

SERVES 2 to 3 depending on the size of the pheasant.

Pigeons with Tangerines

For country people with access to pigeons, this is the way to make them taste more exciting.

    2 onions
    5 tablespoons butter
    chopped parsley and chervil
    the pigeons' livers
    1 stalk celery
    1 cup cooked rice
    seasoning
    4 pigeons
    3 tangerines
    4 pieces back fat (or lard)
    4 tablespoons Grand Marnier
    2 tablespoons Cognac
    2 tablespoons consommé *or* chicken stock
    1 teaspoon castor sugar

Peel the onions and cut in rings. Melt the butter and cook the onions gently. Add the herbs, chopped livers, chopped celery and rice. Season. Stuff the pigeons with this mixture and a little tangerine rind. Put a piece of back fat over as much of the birds as possible. Brown the pigeons on all sides in butter in an earthenware dish and then flame them with the liqueur. Add the consommé or stock and cover and simmer for about 20 minutes. Season. Sprinkle the tangerine quarters with sugar and add to the pigeons and cook for a further 15 minutes.

SERVES 4.

Turkey Roasted with Port

Superb. Having tasted this you'll never cook turkey any other way – but it is rich.

stuffing
    1 tin unsweetened chestnut purée
    450 g (1 lb) sausage meat
    2 glasses port
    450 g (1 lb) breadcrumbs
    2 eggs
    2 chopped onions
    1 crushed clove garlic
    sage *or* parsley
    salt and pepper

    1 turkey
    1 tablespoon oil
    salt and pepper
    275 ml ($\frac{1}{2}$ pint) port
    flour
    cream

Make the stuffing by first mixing the chestnut and sausage meat. Then stir the port into the breadcrumbs and when they have absorbed the liquor, mix them into the meat. Add the beaten egg and other ingredients. Then stuff the bird and sew him up.

Using a pastry brush, coat the bird with oil. Put him in a roasting pan and sprinkle him generously with salt and pepper. Then pour over the first of several glasses of port. Cook in a hot oven for 20 minutes, then turn the oven down to moderate and cook for a total of 20 minutes per pound. Baste frequently with pan juices and add more port from time to time. Turn the bird if you believe this is the best way to keep the flesh from drying. When all is finally cooked, remove the bird and make the sauce by stirring some flour into the pan, scraping everything up and adding more port and stock made with the giblets. Stir in cream just before serving.

These quantities would be adequate for a $3\frac{3}{4}$ to $5\frac{1}{2}$ kg (8

to 12 lb) bird. You can with a bigger bird stuff the other
end with something else – say sage and onion, in which
case don't put sage into the chestnut and port stuffing. It
will be good.

Fish-stuffed Marrows

A fairly cheap, rather unusual dish for the marrow season.

> 2 small *or* 1 medium marrow
> 50 g (2 oz) breadcrumbs
> 1 sherry-glass white wine
> 125 g (4 oz) cottage cheese
> 1 small tin tuna fish
> 1 tablespoon chopped parsley
> oil
> lemon quarters for garnish

Slice the marrows lengthways and boil in salted water until
they are three quarters cooked – the time depends on size
and toughness – say, 5 minutes. Drain thoroughly and
scoop out the seeds. Soak the breadcrumbs in the wine and
stir in the cottage cheese, drained and flaked tuna fish
and the parsley. Mix well. Stand the marrows on aluminium
foil, stuff them with the fish mixture, brush with oil and bake
in a moderate oven for about 30 minutes. Serve with lemon
quarters.

SERVES 2, or 4 as a starter.

Cod Mousse

*A very inexpensive dish, particularly suitable for a buffet
supper.*

> 900 g (2 lb) cod
> salt
> fennel
> 150 ml (¼ pint) mayonnaise

1 lemon jelly
190 ml (⅓ pint) white wine
4 tablespoons vinegar
1 small cucumber

Poach the cod in boiling water with a little salt and fennel. Leave until cold, then take off the skin and flake the flesh into a large bowl. Stir in the mayonnaise.

Add just enough boiling water to the jelly to make it dissolve. When it has cooled, stir in the wine and vinegar.

Peel and slice the cucumber. Pour a little jelly into the bottom of a mould. Then add a layer of cucumber. Leave until set. Stir the rest of the jelly into the fish mixture, then layer with the cucumber slices ending with the cucumber. Leave in the fridge overnight. Turn out and serve with mayonnaise and salad.

N.B. This must be made with proper mayonnaise. If you find the taste of the lemon jelly too sweet it can easily be made with lemon juice and gelatine.

The quantities are not rigid – much depends on the liquidity of your mayonnaise. Try not to make the mixture too sloppy but disaster does not ensue if it is.

SERVES 4 to 6.

Cider Herrings

Cheap and good.

4 herrings
seasoning
1 small chopped onion
1 chopped apple
parsley
chives
thyme
butter
275 ml (½ pint) cider
a dash of lemon juice

Remove the bones from the herrings, clean and lay flat, or ask your fishmonger nicely to do it for you. Season the inside of the fish and sprinkle with chopped onion, chopped apple and some parsley, chives, and thyme. Roll up the fish. Butter a fireproof dish well and lay the fish in it. Pour the cider on top and add the lemon juice. Bake in a fairly slow oven for about 45 minutes.

SERVES 2 or 4 depending on size of herring and the appetite.

Cod Brittany

Cod is so good and cheap but sadly underrated. You'll enjoy this.

    2 tablespoons cooking oil
    900 g (2 lb) fresh cod, boned and skinned
    seasoning
    2 shallots
    125 g (4 oz) mushrooms
    1 teaspoon chopped parsley
    275 ml ($\frac{1}{2}$ pint) cider
    1 tablespoon butter
    1 teaspoon flour

Grease a baking dish with oil, or butter it if preferred, and lay the fish in it. Season. Chop the shallots and mushrooms and sprinkle over the top with the parsley. Pour over the cider. Blend the butter and flour to a smooth paste and add. Cook the fish in a fairly hot oven, basting several times, for about 30 minutes.

SERVES 4.

Haddock Mousse

Delicious for buffet suppers.

> 900 g (2 lb) smoked haddock
> 275 ml (½ pint) milk
> 1 bay leaf
> 1 chopped onion
> whole black peppercorns
> 75 g (3 oz) butter
> 75 g (3 oz) flour
> 150 ml (¼ pint) white wine
> 5 eggs
> 275 ml (½ pint) double cream, lightly whipped

Soak the haddock in cold water for at least 30 minutes. Warm the milk with the bay leaf, chopped onion and peppercorns and poach the fish for 5 minutes. Remove the fish on to a flat plate and leave it to cool. Strain the liquid and reserve 150 ml (¼ pint) of it.

Meanwhile make a sauce with the butter, flour, white wine and fishy milk. While that is cooling, remove all the skin and bones from the flesh of the fish and then mash it with a fork.

By this time the sauce should be cool. Separate the eggs and beat in the yolks one by one. When the sauce is smooth again stir in the fish. Keep stirring until it is smooth. Then stir in the cream. Whip the egg whites until they are stiff and fold them into the fish. Then pour the mousse into a serving dish and leave to cool, preferably overnight.

This can be served from the dish or turned out.

SERVES 6.

Shrimps in a Sherry Sauce

This recipe must be made with fresh shrimps.

> 16 jumbo shrimps, uncooked
> freshly ground black pepper
> salt

175 g (6 oz) butter
1 generous glass sherry
3 egg yolks
275 ml (½ pint) double cream
cooked rice
cayenne
chopped parsley
slices of lemon

Cut the shrimps in half lengthways and season well. Melt some butter in a saucepan and toss the shrimps in this. Add the sherry and reduce. When the liquid has almost boiled away, remove from the heat, add the yolks and cream previously mixed together. Stir well and return to a low heat being careful not to let it boil. When the mixture has thickened, pour it over a bed of cooked rice, and sprinkle with cayenne and chopped parsley. Serve with slices of lemon.

SERVES 4.

Lobster in Cream

Never having met anyone except fishermen and chefs who can watch a lobster being boiled alive, I am afraid that the only recipe I give is for frozen lobster.

125 g (4 oz) butter
1¾ kg (4 lb) lobster meat
seasoning
paprika
2 tablespoons warmed brandy
2 egg yolks
4 tablespoons sherry
1 large carton cream

Melt the butter and gently fry the sliced lobster meat with the seasonings for a couple of minutes. Pour on the brandy, set it alight and shake the pan until the flame dies. Beat the egg yolks and sherry into the cream. Pour this over the meat and warm through until the sauce thickens. Stir all the time and don't let it boil.

SERVES 4 richly.

Mackerel Niçoise

> 2 large *or* 4 smaller mackerel
> 2 tablespoons olive oil
> 25 g (1 oz) butter
> 1 large chopped onion
> 2 crushed cloves garlic
> 150 ml ($\frac{1}{4}$ pint) dry white wine (cider will do)
> 1 dessertspoon tomato purée
> pinch of saffron (if you can get it)
> salt and pepper
> 225 g (8 oz) tomatoes
> parsley
> 12 stoned olives
> 1 sliced lemon

Get your fishmonger to clean the mackerel and take out as many bones as possible. If you have large fish and are using one for two people split them down the back bone which you then remove.

Heat the oil and butter in a large pan, add the onion and garlic and cook gently until they are soft. Put the fish on top and cook for a couple of minutes. Then pour in the wine, tomato purée and seasoning, stir, cover and cook — still gently — for 10 minutes. Take the fish out of the pan and arrange them prettily on a dish. Keep warm.

Reduce the pan juices by boiling vigorously for a couple of minutes. Skin the tomatoes by plunging them briefly into boiling water. Take the pips out and chop them up. Add to the pan and cook gently until the tomatoes are hot. Taste to see if it needs more pepper.

Pour the sauce over the fish, sprinkle with parsley, decorate with olives and lemon.

SERVES 4.

Mackerel with Gooseberry Sauce

Mackerel is a cheap good fish, sadly rather ignored. This is an inexpensive summer supper dish.

   450 g (1 lb) gooseberries
   2 tablespoons cider
   75 g (3 oz) butter
   1 tablespoon sugar (or more to taste)
   4 small or 2 large mackerel, filleted
   seasoned flour
   juice of 1 small lemon
   few sprigs of parsley

Wash the gooseberries. Stew them in the cider and 25 g (1 oz) butter until they are soft. Liquidize and sieve them (if you've no liquidizer force them through a sieve with a wooden spoon – a tedious process which will soon force you to buy a liquidizer!). Stir in the sugar and warm through until the mixture thickens. This is meant to be tart so don't add too much sugar.

   Meanwhile dip the mackerel fillets in seasoned flour. (Unless you arrive at your fishmonger at the rush hour he will fillet your fish for you, if he won't, change your fishmonger.) Melt the remaining butter in a frying pan. Cook the fish for about 7 minutes turning once. Remove and keep warm. Continue to heat the butter until it browns, then take off the heat, add the lemon juice and parsley and pour over the fish. Serve the hot sauce separately.

SERVES 4.

Plaice with Shrimps and Wine

A likeable dish which can be made the day before – just put it under a hot grill when you want it.

   8 fillets plaice
   seasoned flour
   butter

275 ml ($\frac{1}{2}$ pint) dry white wine
2 shallots *or* $\frac{1}{2}$ small onion
1 carton double cream
125 g (4 oz) button mushrooms
25 g (1 oz) Parmesan
1 small packet frozen shrimps *or* 1 small tin, drained

Roll up the fish and coat with seasoned flour. Melt the butter and brown the fish on all sides. Butter a fireproof dish well and place the fish in it. Pour over the wine and bake for about 20 minutes in a moderate oven.

Meanwhile finely chop the shallots and fry in butter until very soft. Stir in the remains of the seasoned flour and cook for a few seconds more. Pour in the cream and boil for a minute. In another pan cook the mushrooms in the minimum of water or butter. Add them to the sauce together with the grated cheese, shrimps and the drained liquid from the cooked fish. Pour the finished sauce over the fish and brown under a hot grill for a few minutes before serving.

SERVES 4 as a main course, 8 as a starter.

Plaice with Vermouth Sauce

This excellent recipe can be adapted to most fish and can hardly fail.

4 fillets of plaice (*or* sole if you can afford them)
175 g (6 oz) butter
6 tablespoons dry Vermouth
1 teaspoon tomato purée
salt and pepper
1 small carton single cream
few sprigs of chopped parsley

Butter a casserole. Arrange the rolled fillets in it. Melt the butter and stir in the Vermouth and tomato purée. Pour the sauce over the fish and bake in a hot oven for 30 minutes or until the fish flakes when touched with a fork.

Add the cream and shake the pan vigorously. Sprinkle with parsley and serve.

SERVES 4.

Braised Salmon in White Wine

14 g ($\frac{1}{2}$ oz) butter
1 onion
900 g–1$\frac{1}{3}$ kg (2–3 lb) piece of salmon
$\frac{1}{2}$ bottle dry white wine
salt and pepper
bouquet garni
sauce:
4 egg yolks
225 g (8 oz) butter
lemon juice
seasoning

Butter a large baking dish. Finely slice the onion over the bottom, lay the clean salmon on top. Cover with the wine, sprinkle with salt and pepper and add bouquet garni. Place a buttered piece of paper over the fish, cover the dish with foil and cook in a moderate oven for about 30 minutes.

Remove the skin and place the salmon on a serving dish. Keep warm.

Strain the wine and juices into a fresh pan and boil until reduced by half. Meanwhile gently melt the butter in another pan. In yet another pan whisk the egg yolks and strained juices over a very low heat, until they thicken. Remove from the heat, whisk in the butter very slowly and add a squeeze of lemon juice. Taste and add more seasoning if necessary. Don't overheat.

SERVES 6.

Salmon Mousse

    425 ml (¾ pint) aspic jelly
    350 g (12 oz) cooked salmon
    salt and pepper
    paprika
    2 tablespoons sherry
    275 ml (½ pint) cream
    hard-boiled egg, cucumber, green pepper *or* tomato to
        decorate

Make the aspic jelly and allow to cool. Bone the fish and
mash with a fork or put in an electric mixer gently.
Gradually stir in 150 ml (¼ pint) cold jelly, seasoning and
sherry. Fold in the lightly whisked cream. Pour into a serving dish, smooth the surface with the back of a spoon and
leave in the fridge to cool. Pour on a quarter-inch of aspic
jelly, return to the fridge. Decorate with egg or cucumber or
whatever and cover with the remaining jelly. Allow to set.

SERVES 4.

Seafood Fennel

Delicious for fennel fanciers.

    6 scallops
    150 ml (¼ pint) milk
    25 g (1 oz) butter
    25 g (1 oz) flour
    150 ml (¼ pint) white wine
    tin plain crabmeat
    175 g (6 oz) peeled prawns *or* scampi
    4 fennel
    150 ml (¼ pint) sour cream
    breadcrumbs
    grated cheese

Remove the orange part from the scallops and slice the
white parts into two. Poach them in the milk for about 15
minutes. Remove the fish. Melt the butter, stir in the flour

and using the fishy milk make a béchamel sauce. Add the wine and cook for a little longer. Meanwhile, drain the crabmeat, remove the bones and flake the fish. Add to the sauce with the prawns and scallops including orange parts and stir well. Keep warm. Slice the fennel and boil in salted water for about 10 minutes (the exact time depends upon the size of fennel. When cooked but not slushy, drain well, toss in butter and spread on the bottom of a serving dish. Stir the sour cream into the fish and pour it over the top. Sprinkle the lot with breadcrumbs and grated cheese and pop under a hot grill for a minute or so.

SERVES 6.

Rare beings who don't like fennel can substitute celery, chicory or even broccoli.

Scallops in Sherry Sauce

Scallops traditionally are cooked in a sauce and then returned to their shells in which they are served. If the shells are flat and the contents spill out, serve them in individual ovenproof dishes instead.

    6 scallops
    275 ml (½ pint) sweet sherry
    275 ml (½ pint) water
    bouquet garni
    1 fillet fresh haddock
    14 g (½ oz) butter
    14 g (½ oz) flour
    seasoning

Cut the orange parts away from the scallops. Poach the whites gently in the sherry, water and bouquet garni for 10 minutes. Then add the chopped orange parts and the haddock and cook for a further 5 minutes. Remove the fish and keep warm. Boil the bouillon vigorously until it is reduced by half. Meanwhile skin the haddock and slice it; slice the scallops, still keeping warm. Dissolve the butter, stir in the flour and seasoning, cook for 1 minute and add the reduced bouillon. Divide the fish between four shells and pour sauce over. Keep very hot until required.

SERVES 4 as a main course, or 6 (in six shells) as a starter.

This can also be made with white wine in which case it is much lighter, or with 550 ml (1 pint) cider omitting the water.

Scampi with Mushroom and Cream Sauce

This is a perfect dish to produce when you want to do something good in a hurry.

> 450 g (1 lb) frozen scampi (thawed)
> seasoned flour
> 50 g (2 oz) butter
> 125 g (4 oz) perfect button mushrooms, sliced
> 2 glasses white wine
> $\frac{1}{2}$ small carton double cream
> few sprigs chopped parsley

Dip the scampi in seasoned flour. Heat the butter. Gently fry the scampi for about 10 minutes. (If you are the kind of cook who invariably burns butter, use a little less and add a drop or two of good oil instead, it won't affect the flavour and ought to stop the burning.) Add the mushrooms and the wine and cook for about another 15 minutes. Then add the cream, cook until it is heated through but not boiling. Sprinkle with parsley before serving with plain boiled rice.

SERVES 4.

Baked Fillet of Sole

Excellent and easy.

1 tablespoon butter
1 teaspoon flour
125 g (4 oz) mushrooms
2 shallots
1 teaspoon chopped chives
1 tablespoon chopped parsley
breadcrumbs
8 fillets of sole
grated Swiss cheese
½ cup white wine
chicken stock

Cream the butter with the flour and spread on a shallow baking dish. Mix together the finely chopped mushrooms and shallots, chives and parsley. Spread half this mixture on the baking dish and sprinkle with fine breadcrumbs. Arrange the rolled sole on the top. Cover the fish with the remaining vegetables. Sprinkle lightly again with a few breadcrumbs and a little grated cheese. Dot with butter. Add the wine and a little chicken stock and bake in a moderate oven for about 25 minutes.

SERVES 4.

Tuna Quiche

Quite a substantial supper dish, easily prepared and very good.

175 g (6 oz) shortcrust pastry
200 g (7 oz) tin tuna fish
125 g (4 oz) grated hard cheese
1 egg
90 ml (3 oz) milk
dash of medium sherry
freshly ground black pepper

Roll out the pastry to line a 15-cm (6-inch) flan dish. Drain the oil off the tuna fish. With a fork flake the fish in a large bowl and mix it with the grated cheese. Beat the egg with the milk and pour it into the fish mixture with the sherry and pepper. Stir well. Fill the flan with the fish and bake in a hot oven for 25 minutes.

You can substitute cream or evaporated milk for the egg-and-milk mixture but they work out more expensive and little better.

Serve this hot with vegetables or cold with salad. Even so, re-warm the quiche for 10 minutes before eating: it's rather nasty straight from the fridge.

SERVES 4.

Puddings

Delicious Apple Dessert

This is ridiculously easy and so good.

900 g (2 lb) apples
sugar
1 tablespoon Calvados
150 ml (¼ pint) double cream *or* more
50 g (2 oz) dark chocolate

Stew the peeled and sliced apples in a little water. When cooked sweeten to taste (not too much sugar). Then sieve. When cool stir in the Calvados. Pour into a serving dish. Whip the cream until thick, spread over the apple mixture and then leave in the fridge for several hours. Just before eating sprinkle thickly with grated chocolate.

SERVES 4 or more.

This can be expanded by lining the dish with boudoir biscuits soaked in Calvados.

French Apple Omelette

This is so good that having discovered the recipe I made it three times in four days and still enjoyed it when a friend served it to me, as a great surprise, on the fifth day.

4 to 7 eggs
salt
5 tablespoons castor sugar
5 tablespoons butter
2 peeled, cored and sliced apples
3 tablespoons double cream
2 tablespoons Calvados *or* Kirsch
2 more tablespoons liquor for firing

Beat the eggs with a pinch of salt and a little of the sugar.
Melt half the butter, add the apples and cook very gently until they are soft. Then add the cream, liquor and the rest of the sugar. Keep the mixture warm.

Heat the rest of the butter in a good omelette pan. When hot enough add the eggs and cook. When the omelette is all but done, spread the apple mixture over half of it. Fold it over and slip it out on to a warmed dish, sprinkle with sugar and liquor. Set fire and serve immediately.

SERVES 4 to 5 depending on the amount of eggs.

(You can use cooking apples but if so add a little more sugar with the cream.)

Apples Baked with Rum and Apricot Jam

With a family resemblance to everybody's favourite nursery food, apples baked this way are more popular than ever.

> 8 tablespoons apricot jam
> 1 glass rum
> 125 g (4 oz) raisins
> 8 large apples
> butter
> nutmeg

Put the apricot jam, rum and raisins in a bowl and mix together. Core the apples and wipe them clean. Rub a little butter on them and fill them with the fruit mixture. Sprinkle them with nutmeg and wrap in lightly buttered tin foil. Bake in a hot oven in a flat dish for about 20 minutes.

SERVES 8.

This can also be made with the runny stuff left at the bottom of the marmalade jar after all the greedy people have eaten the chunky bits.

Apples Stewed in Cider

This is simplicity itself and much nicer than ordinary stewed apples. It's an ideal light pudding at the end of a roast meat and two veg. meal and can be cooked in the same oven.

900 g (2 lb) apples (cooking *or* eating)
brown sugar
275 ml ($\frac{1}{2}$ pint) cider

Peel and slice the apples. Put them into a suitable dish. Add brown sugar – quite a lot if you use cooking apples, less if not. Add the cider.

Cover the dish and bake for about 30 minutes in a moderate oven. Then baste the apples, uncover and cook for a further 10 minutes. Serve hot or cold, ideally with thick cream.

SERVES 4 to 6.

Toffee Apple Oats

Rather substantial, rather good.

75 g (3 oz) butter
75 g (3 oz) brown sugar
75 g (3 oz) oats
675 g (1 lb 8 oz) cooking apples
small carton double cream
1 tablespoon Calvados
25 g (1 oz) grated dark chocolate

Melt the butter. Stir in the brown sugar and oats, mixing thoroughly. Leave to cool. Stew the cooking apples until soft, sieve and allow to cool. Layer the sticky oats and apples as many times as possible, ending with oats. Whip the cream with the Calvados and spread over the top. Decorate with grated chocolate.

SERVES 4.

Hot Apricot Soufflé

Not fattening as soufflés go, and not complicated either.

    1 large tin apricots
    1 dessertspoon Kirsch
    3 egg whites
    1 heaped tablespoon castor sugar

Thoroughly drain the apricots and liquidize them with the Kirsch. Whisk the egg whites in a large bowl, then add the sugar and whisk a little longer. Fold the fruit purée into the egg whites. Pour into a buttered soufflé dish and immediately bake in a moderate oven for 10 minutes or until golden.

SERVES 3.

Apricots Sweet and Sour

    450 g (1 lb) stoned apricots
    juice of 1 orange
    5-cm (2-inch) cinnamon stick
    75 g (3 oz) sugar
    1 tablespoon brandy *or* apricot liqueur
    1 small carton sour cream
    50 g (2 oz) soft brown sugar
    25 g (1 oz) ground almonds

Cook the apricots with the orange juice, cinnamon and sugar until soft. Pour into a small soufflé dish with the liqueur. Cool. Cover with the sour cream. Mix the brown sugar with the almonds and sprinkle over the cream. Put under a hot grill until the sugar caramelizes. Chill.

SERVES 4.

Apricot Ice Cream Pudding

This can be made well in advance.

>   1 975 ml (34 fl oz) Cornish ice cream (there'll be some left over)
>   50 g (2 oz) finely chopped blanched almonds
>   425 g (15 oz) tin apricots
>   3 tablespoons brandy

Let the ice cream soften a little, and then mix in the almonds. Line a 550-ml (1-pint) pudding basin with the ice cream, being careful to cover the bottom and sides well, with two-thirds of the mixture. (It may help to put the basin in the freezer for a few minutes halfway through this process if the ice cream is not being co-operative.) Freeze for a few minutes before adding the drained apricots and the brandy. Cover the top with the remaining ice cream and freeze until needed. Turn out and decorate with a few more chopped nuts if required. Serve fast.

SERVES 4 to 6.

Apricot and Orange Fool

A refreshing, slightly tart dessert of which I am very fond.

>   1 large tin apricots
>   3 oranges
>   275 ml ($\frac{1}{2}$ pint) double cream
>   3 tablespoons apricot brandy – or orange liqueur

Gently stew the apricots and oranges for about 30 minutes. Don't let the mixture stick. If there is a lot of juice reserve it. Liquidize the fruit, skins and all. When it is cool stir in enough of the liquid to make the purée like thick cream. Gently whip the cream (it doesn't want to be stiff), and fold it in with the liqueur. Either pour into a large glass bowl or individual serving dishes.

SERVES 6.

Banana Cream

A light and refreshing way of serving bananas. Dislikers of yoghurt would never detect its existence.

> 6 medium bananas
> 4 cartons natural yoghurt
> sugar to taste if yoghurt is not sweetened
> 3 tablespoons white wine
> 1 tablespoon lemon juice

If you have a liquidizer, blend all the ingredients together and turn into serving bowl. Chill.

If you haven't a liquidizer, mash the bananas first and then stir in everything else. Some people decorate this with fine slices of another banana. This must be done at the last minute or it will brown.

SERVES 6.

Flambéed Bananas

> 8 bananas
> ¼ cup water
> 1 good tablespoon lemon juice
> butter
> 8 tablespoons sugar
> 3 tablespoons brandy
> whipped cream

Peel the bananas and lay them in a fireproof dish. Sprinkle with water and the lemon juice. Cover each banana with several dots of butter and a tablespoon of sugar. Bake in a moderate oven for about 20 minutes, basting a couple of times. Warm the brandy, light it and pour over the bananas just before serving. Shake the dish until the flame goes out. Serve with whipped cream.

SERVES 4.

Extra Special Blackberry and Apple Mousse

This I find delicious and refreshing.

> 450 g (1 lb) cooking apples
> a little water
> 225 g (8 oz) blackberries
> 125 g (4 oz) castor sugar
> 1 envelope gelatine
> 2 egg whites
> 2 tablespoons Calvados

Wash and peel the apples, cutting into quarters. Put them into a pan with a little water, the washed blackberries and most of the sugar. Stew gently until the fruit is pulpy. Then liquidize and strain into a large serving dish. Dissolve the gelatine in a little water and stir it into the fruit. When all is cold, whisk the egg white until stiff and fold into the fruit purée with the remaining sugar and the Calvados. Chill until required.

SERVES 6.

Cherry Meringue

Simple, and a nice show-off if you have cherry trees.

> 900 g (2 lb) cherries
> 50 to 225 g (2 to 8 oz) granulated sugar (depending on
>   the tartness of the cherries)
> 2 tablespoons cherry brandy
> 2 egg whites
> 125 g (4 oz) castor sugar

Wash the cherries and remove stalks and stones. Gently stew them for 5 minutes with the sugar and just enough water to cover. Take the cherries out of the pan and boil the juice until it is reduced to a half. Stir in the cherry brandy.

Put the cherries and juice into a soufflé dish. Beat the egg whites until stiff and fold in most of the castor sugar.

Beat again. Spread this meringue mixture over the fruit, sprinkle with the remaining castor sugar and bake in a moderate oven for about 10 minutes, until it is a lovely golden brown. I like it hot but it can be served cold as well.

SERVES 4 to 6.

Black Cherry Tipsy Trifle

This can't be made too far in advance (say, more than 24 hours) as it gets soggy, but as it takes so little time, it can be made at a moment's notice, though the sultanas are better if soaked for a while.

> 125 g (4 oz) sultanas
> 4 tablespoons cherry brandy
> 2 packets Lyons' Trifle sponges (2 for a wide open dish or 1 if a soufflé dish is used)
> 2 tins black cherries
> 125 g (4 oz) flaked almonds
> 275 ml (½ pint) double cream

Pour the cherry brandy over the sultanas and leave in a jar for several hours. Slice the sponge cakes lengthwise and line a large bowl with them. Strain the cherries keeping juice. Sprinkle the cake with less than half the juice – do not make the cake too soggy. Spread the cherries over the cake, leaving out a few to decorate the trifle. Add the sultanas in brandy and almonds. Whip the cream until nearly stiff. Spread over the pudding. Leave in the fridge for at least 1 hour. (If the pudding is made the day before, add cream before serving.) Decorate with the remaining cherries.

SERVES 6 to 8.

Cherry Wine Delight

    675 g (1 lb 8 oz) black cherries
    3 glasses red wine
    cinnamon
    2 cloves
    50 g (2 oz) sugar
    2 tablespoons redcurrant jelly
    275 ml (½ pint) double cream
    1½ tablespoons brandy
    25 g (1 oz) castor sugar

Wash the cherries and remove the stones and stalks. Stew
them until soft with the wine, a good pinch of cinnamon,
the cloves and the sugar. Remove the cherries and put them
in the serving dish to cool. Boil the juice until reduced and
fairly thick. Remove the cloves and stir in the redcurrant
jelly. Pour over the fruit. Set aside to cool. Whip the cream
with the brandy and sugar and pile on top of the cherries.

SERVES 4.

Chestnut Chocolate

*Good, rich and much admired, also extremely easy to
make.*

    75 g (3 oz) butter
    75 g (3 oz) castor sugar
    175 g (6 oz) dark chocolate
    1 425 g (15 oz) tin unflavoured, unsweetened chestnut
      purée
    3 tablespoons rum *or* brandy
    1 large carton best thick cream (ideally Marks and
      Spencer Channel Island)

Beat the butter, add the sugar little by little and continue
beating until at least a little lighter than when you started.
Meanwhile melt the chocolate in the minimum of water.
Beat with a wooden spoon until all lumps disappear. Allow

to cool. Beat the chestnut purée into the butter cream, stir
in the rum or brandy and the cooled chocolate. Butter a
loaf tin and pour the mixture in. Leave in the fridge overnight. Turn out. Slice and serve with dollops of thick cream.

SERVES 8, or even more if previous courses have been
filling.

Chestnut Cream

The oranges are a terrific asset to the flavour.

> oranges – number depending on size of dish
> 275 ml (½ pint) cream
> 2 tablespoons brandy
> 1 tin chestnut purée
> icing sugar
> 2 egg whites
> chopped nuts

Line the whole of a glass dish with thin slices of orange
(cut across the fruit). Whip the cream with the brandy and
stir in the chestnut purée, adding the sugar to taste. Whisk
the egg whites until stiff and fold into the chestnut mixture.
Pour this into the glass dish and decorate with slices of
orange on top. Sprinkle with chopped nuts and chill.

SERVES 6 to 8 – it is rich.

Flambéed Figs

A very light dessert to end off a substantial meal.

> 12 ripe figs
> 3 tablespoons orange liqueur
> 3 tablespoons brandy
> 275 ml (½ pint) whipped cream

Carefully peel the figs and prick: they must stay whole.

Arrange them in a fireproof dish. Warm the orange liqueur and brandy in a ladle over a flame and then pour it over the figs. Set the liquor alight and gently shake the dish until the flame goes out. Serve at once with whipped cream.

SERVES 6.

Fruit Posset

If you ever need to make a very good sweet in a hurry this one can get you out of a difficult hole – providing you have a good store cupboard and can lay hands on cream.

    any 225 g (8 oz) tin soft fruit
    275 ml ($\frac{1}{2}$ pint) double cream
    1 tablespoon Kirsch
    chopped nuts for decoration

Sieve the fruit and mash it with a fork. Whip the cream until only fairly thick. Stir in the fruit and liqueur and put in the freezer for 30 minutes or so. Take out and put in the fridge at the beginning of the meal so that it is not too hard by the time you need it. Sprinkle with chopped nuts before serving.

SERVES 3 to 4.

This has endless permutations; match the fruit to the liqueur, use fresh fruit in summer, use sweet port with loganberries. At a pinch you can just about get away with tinned cream but I would use a little more liqueur to mask the taste.

Instant Fruit Mousse

No trouble, no effort and tastes remarkably good.

    1 tin strawberries
    1 packet strawberry jelly

1 tin evaporated milk
3 tablespoons Kirsch
1 small carton double cream
50 g (2 oz) chopped walnuts

Strain the fruit reserving the juice. Melt the jelly in the fruit juice. Whip the milk until it is frothy. Mash the fruit with a fork and whip that in as well. Stir in the jelly and the Kirsch. Mix well. Pour into a serving bowl and leave in a cool place to set. Then whip the cream until thick and spread over the top of the dessert. Decorate with finely chopped walnuts.

SERVES 6 to 8.

This can equally be made with raspberries, raspberry jelly and Kirsch, 2 tins of mandarins, tangerine jelly and Cointreau or plums, lemon jelly and sherry.

Fruit Salad

There are no laws for fruit salads. You put into them whatever is in season and you like. Mine never have bananas. If you put the juice of the first lemon into the bowl in which you are making the salad, and toss apples, etc., as you chop them up, they won't go brown.

2 lemons
2 tablespoons sugar or more if you are sweet-toothed
150 ml (¼ pint) water
3 oranges
3 apples
2 pears
2 tablespoons Cointreau

Grate the rind of the lemons into a pan. Squeeze the lemons, dividing the juice between the pan and the bowl in which you are preparing the salad. Add the sugar, water and juice of 1 orange to the pan and boil gently for 5 minutes. Peel and finely slice the rest of the fruit and toss in the lemon juice in the bowl. Add the strained syrup and the liqueur.

SERVES 4.

The variations are enormous. Kirsch is good especially with pineapple. Crème de Menthe is excellent with apples and any exotic fruit liqueur goes with its own fruit.

Norwegian Fruit Salad

    12 oranges
    12 apples
    1 pineapple
    1 cup chopped walnuts
    sugar to taste
    juice of 6 oranges
    1 cup dry sherry

Slice and peel the oranges. Core the apples, but do not peel, and cut into thin slices. (Both these should be sliced the width of the fruit.) Cut the pineapple into pieces. Put the fruit in a bowl together with the nuts, sugar and add the juice of the other 6 oranges. Chill. Just before serving add the sherry. Serve with boudoir biscuits.

SERVES 12.

Sherbet and Champagne Fruit Cup

An extravagant, mouth-watering dessert for very special occasions.

    enough fresh diced mixed fruit for 8 people, i.e. pine-
      apple, apples, bananas, strawberries, oranges and
      seedless grapes
    4 tablespoons sugar
    3 tablespoons Kirsch

1 teaspoon of lemon sherbet per person
8 sprigs of mint
½ bottle chilled champagne

Fill individual glasses with the fresh fruit. Sprinkle with the sugar and Kirsch. Chill. Add a dollop of lemon sherbet and a sprig of mint to each glass. At the table, open the champagne and pour over the fruit (drink any remains!).

SERVES 8.

Grapefruit Cheesecake

The grapefruit gives this otherwise rather rich cake a very refreshing flavour

275 g (10 oz) digestive biscuits
nutmeg
cinnamon
175 g (6 oz) butter
2 grapefruit
2 eggs
140 g (4½ oz) sugar
salt
75 ml (⅛ pint) grapefruit juice
1 teaspoon gelatine
350 g (12 oz) cream cheese
½ teaspoon each of grated lemon rind and grapefruit rind
1 dessertspoon lemon juice
1 tablespoon Kirsch *or* more
150 ml (¼ pint) double cream

Either crush the biscuits with a wooden spoon or put in a blender. Add a good pinch of both spices. Melt the butter and mix into the biscuit crumbs. Press the mixture around the sides and bottom of a 20-cm (8-inch) tin or Pyrex dish. Chill.

Peel the grapefruit and skin the sections, reserving the juice. Keep about 6 pieces for decorating the top. Cut the rest into small pieces. Separate one egg and put aside the white. In a double saucepan beat the yolk and the other whole egg, sugar, salt and a tablespoon of grapefruit juice. Stir over gentle heat until it thickens. Cool. Dissolve the gelatine in a quarter of a cup of cold water and add to the custard. Cool. Blend the cream cheese with the remaining grapefruit juice, fruit rinds and lemon juice and Kirsch. Gradually beat into the custard. Fold the cut-up grapefruit segments into the stiffly whipped cream and the stiffly whipped egg white. Mix with the custard. Pour the mixture into the biscuit case and decorate with the whole grapefruit segments on top. Chill.

SERVES 8.

Cold Lemon Soufflé

The only difficulty about cold soufflés is to mix the gelatine really thoroughly into the cream mixture. If this isn't done the consistency is wrong and the whole thing is spoilt. It's not hard, just takes persistence.

    3 eggs
    225 g (8 oz) castor sugar
    2 large lemons
    1 envelope gelatine
    2 tablespoons Cointreau *or* Grand Marnier
    275 ml (½ pint) double cream
    toasted coconut *or* finely chopped almonds

First wrap some aluminium foil round the soufflé dish – it must stand up at least two inches above the top of the dish. Tie it on with string.

Separate the eggs. In a large mixing bowl whisk the yolks, sugar, grated rind and juice of the lemons until they are pale yellow and thick.

Soften the gelatine in the liqueur and warm it gently until it dissolves completely. Thoroughly mix the gelatine into the lemon mixture. Then whisk the cream until it thickens, the egg whites until they are stiff and fold them both into the lemon. When this begins to set (which will be very soon) pour the whole lot into the prepared soufflé dish. Chill. Before serving peel off the foil and decorate the sides and top with the coconut or nuts.

SERVES 6.

Lemon Syllabub

Frequently served by doctors and dentists who don't know what else to do with the sweet sherry their patients give them. It's gorgeous.

> 1 large carton double cream
> 1 Sherry-glass sweet sherry
> grated rind and juice of 1 lemon
> castor sugar to taste

Whip up all the ingredients together and chill before serving.

SERVES 3 to 4.

Rum and Lemon Sorbet

This sorbet is refreshing and good for summer lunches in the garden. (It can tolerate standing around in the sun for a while being so hard and inedible when it comes out of the freezer.) If to be eaten on other occasions, take out of the freezer and store in the fridge for an hour or so before needed.

> 125 g (4 oz) granulated sugar
> 275 ml ($\frac{1}{2}$ pint) water
> the rind and juice of 1 large lemon
> the juice of 1 orange
> 1 tablespoon rum
> 1 egg white

Heat the sugar and water gently until the sugar dissolves.

Continue cooking for another 10 minutes. Finely chop the rind and stir it into the syrup. Leave to cool. When cold stir in the fruit juices and strain into a clean bowl. Keep in the freezer until almost frozen.

Then decant into another bowl, stir in the rum and fold in a stiffly beaten egg white. Freeze until solid.

SERVES 4.

Mandarin Gâteau

Make a day or so in advance for best effect – it's rich, so please serve after a fairly light course.

> 200 g (7 oz) butter
> 175 g (6 oz) castor sugar
> 25 g (1 oz) flour
> 150 ml ($\frac{1}{4}$ pint) milk
> 2 small tins mandarin oranges
> 1 egg
> about 20 boudoir biscuits (less than 2 packets) depending on size of mould
> 8 tablespoons port
> 1 large carton double cream
> packet of chocolate finger biscuits (optional)
> toasted almonds

Cream 175 g (6 oz) of the butter and the sugar together until they are very pale and frothy. This can be tedious even with an electric beater, some help can be gained by using butter which has been out of the fridge for an hour or two. Make a white sauce with the other 25 g (1 oz) of butter, the flour and the milk. Over a low heat stir in the strained juice from one of the tins of mandarins. Off the heat beat in the egg. Cover and cool.

Mash the mandarins from that tin with a fork, and slowly beat them into the butter and sugar mixture with the sauce.

Dip each sponge finger in the port and then line the base of a plastic box 25 by 12½ cm (10 by 5 in) (or 30 by 5 cm

(12 by 2 in), or 20 by 10 cm (8 by 4 in) or similar). Spread half the filling over this layer. Dip the remaining fingers in the remaining port and layer again. Cover with the drained fruit from the second tin. Spread the rest of the filling over this and chill. Before serving whip the cream until fairly thick. Put a serving dish over the mould, turn it upside down and shake the dessert out. Cover with a very thin layer of cream and then cover the sides with the chocolate biscuits side by side. Spread the rest of the cream on top and sprinkle with chopped toasted almonds.

SERVES 8 plus.

Melon and Pineapple

    1 large honeydew melon
    1 large tin diced pineapple
    1 sherry-glass Kirsch

Slice the top off the melon and keep it. Remove the seeds. Scoop out the flesh and dice it or use a special scoop to make melon balls. Put them in a bowl. Drain the pineapple and mix it with the melon and the Kirsch. Cut a slice off the bottom of the melon so that it will stand upright. Fill the melon shell with the mixture and replace the lid. Wrap well in foil before chilling in the fridge.

SERVES 6.

Minty Melon

This is a little more exciting than serving a quarter of a melon per head; it is marginally more effort but well worth it.

    1 small ripe melon
    2 tablespoons good lime cordial
    150 ml ($\frac{1}{4}$ pint) sweet white wine
    few sprigs chopped mint

Cut the top off the melon, spoon out the seeds and then remove the flesh. Either do so with a little balling device or else remove in large chunks and dice the flesh. When you have taken out as much of the flesh as possible, gently mix in a bowl with the lime, wine and mint. Return to the shell, wrap in foil and leave in the fridge until required. This will happily keep for a day or two.

SERVES 4.

Ginger Melon

This is refreshing, easy and can be prepared well in advance. Do cover the melon in the fridge or smell problems occur.

> 1 canteloupe melon
> 1½ teaspoons powdered ginger
> 125 g (4 oz) castor sugar
> 4 tablespoons brandy *or* rum
> 1 large carton double cream

Cut the melon in half, scoop out the flesh and dice or ball it. Keep the melon shells. Place the melon dice or balls in a bowl with the ginger and sugar. Cover and chill. Before serving, add the brandy and pile into the melon shells. Serve with whipped cream.

SERVES 4 to 6 depending on the size of the melon.

Orange and Grapefruit Caramel

> 2 grapefruit
> 2 oranges
> 2 tablespoons Kirsch or Bols Gin
> soft brown sugar

Peel the fruit and remove all the pith. Skin the segments. Pack them evenly in a bowl and sprinkle with the liqueur and enough brown sugar to cover about a quarter inch thick. Place under a hot grill for a couple of minutes until the sugar caramelizes and either serve hot immediately, or chill it and serve cold. Very good either way.

SERVES 4 to 6.

Orange Fool

And a fool can make this perfect dessert.

4 oranges
2 lemons
550 ml (1 pint) double cream
1 tablespoon of an orange liqueur *or* brandy
8 sponge cakes

Grate the rind of 2 oranges and 1 lemon. Liquidize all the fruit and strain it.

Beat the cream slightly. Add the fruit juice, grated rinds and liqueur. Line the dish in which the pudding is to be served with halved sponge cakes (or boudoir biscuits) and pour the cream over the top. Put in the fridge for at least 24 hours.

SERVES 6.

Orange Salad

This is excellent, easy and everybody loves it.

8 oranges
275 ml (½ pint) water
450 g (1 lb) sugar
Cointreau, Grand Marnier *or* Orange Curaçao to taste

Peel the oranges with a very sharp knife to remove all the pith. (The easiest way is cut off both ends, lay the orange flat on a board and slice the peel off downwards in about 1-inch strips. This removes all the pith and skin together.) Remove the pith from half the rind, and slice the rind into very thin strips. Melt the sugar in the water, stir and bring to the boil. Boil until in a few minutes you have a thickish pale golden syrup. Add the strips of orange peel and continue cooking until almost caramelized. Cool, and add the liqueur. Pour over the oranges and serve chilled – with cream if wished. This should be done a day in advance.

SERVES 4.

Orange Jelly

This is very light and cool – a perfect end to a heavy meal.

> 6 to 10 oranges (depending on size or juiciness)
> orange liqueur to taste
> 1 envelope gelatine

Skin the oranges and put in a liquidizer. Add about 150 ml (5 oz) water. Sieve into the bowl in which the pudding will be served. Add the liqueur. Dissolve the gelatine in a little water. Stir it vigorously into the juice. There must be *no* lumps. Leave to set in a cool place. This will keep for some days and can be served with liqueur-enriched cream or on its own.

SERVES 6.

Hot Orange Soufflé in Orange Skins

This is spectacular to look at, easy to cook and good to eat.

> 6 large oranges plus grated rind of 1 orange
> 25 g (1 oz) butter
> 2 teaspoons flour
> 150 ml (¼ pint) milk
> 4 eggs

1 tablespoon sugar
2 tablespoons Curaçao, Cointreau *or* Grand Marnier

Cut the tops off the oranges at least a quarter way down. Using a rounded grapefruit knife, scoop out all the flesh and pour out the juice. Reserve. Stand the orange skins in tartlet tins to hold them upright. Heat the butter, flour and milk stirring all the time. When thick, beat in the egg yolks, sugar and finely grated orange rind. Then fold in the orange liqueur and the stiffly beaten egg whites. Partly fill the orange skins, sprinkle a little castor sugar evenly over the top and bake in a hot oven for 5 minutes until golden on top.

SERVES 6.

Use the orange flesh to make juice for breakfast.

Hot Caramel Oranges

This is delicious and no harder than grapefruit for breakfast.

4 large oranges (not thick-skinned and much nicer if seedless)
8 teaspoons Cointreau
a little castor sugar

Cut the oranges in half horizontally. Remove the core and loosen the segments with a grapefruit knife. Place, cut-side upwards, in a fireproof dish and pour a teaspoon of the liqueur into each. Cook in a medium oven for about 15 minutes. Remove. Sprinkle a little castor sugar on the surface of each orange and place under a hot grill until the sugar caramelizes to a dark brown. Eat soon.

SERVES 4.

Grilled Grapefruit

This is similar to the previous recipe but not quite so festive looking. Many people serve it as a first course.

2 grapefruit
a little sherry *or* Madeira
brown sugar

Halve the grapefruit and prepare in the usual way loosening all the segments. Sprinkle each half with a little sherry and a thin layer of sugar. Put under a hot grill until the sugar is dissolved and serve immediately.

SERVES 4.

Poached Peaches with Raspberry Sauce

A delicious summer dessert.

8 ripe white peaches
425 ml (¾ pint) water
150 g (5 oz) granulated sugar
vanilla pod
3 punnets fresh raspberries
1 tablespoon Kirsch
blanched chopped almonds

Parboil the peaches for about 1 minute, peel and leave whole. In a separate saucepan, boil the water, sugar and vanilla for a few minutes. Remove the vanilla, and add the peaches and poach in the syrup over a low heat for 5 minutes. Remove to a serving dish. Liquidize 3 cups of fresh raspberries and strain the seeds through a fine sieve. Sweeten the sauce with 2 or 3 tablespoons of the peach syrup and add the Kirsch. Pour over the peaches and chill. Before serving sprinkle with blanched chopped almonds.

SERVES 8.

Peaches with Mincemeat and Whisky

This is an astonishingly good dessert which strains the culinary talent of no man.

> 1 large tin peach halves (about 8 halves)
> 2 tablespoons whisky
> 8 dessertspoons mincemeat
> 8 teaspoons whisky

Drain the juice from the peaches into a pan. Pour about a quarter of it away or drink it. Add two tablespoons of whisky.

Put the peaches, flat side up, in a large serving dish. Into the centre of each put a dessertspoon of mincemeat and a teaspoon of whisky. Just before eating warm the syrup and whisky mixture and pour it over the fruit.

SERVES 4 to 8 depending on whether your guests are hungry.

Peaches in Brandy

First invented on a wet camping holiday when both ingredients were very cheap.

> At least one big peach per head
> sugar
> brandy – very inferior if that's all that's available

Ideally peel the peaches. Slice. Put alternate layers of peach, sugar, ideally castor, and brandy in a container. Leave for as long as you can bear. Serve with thick cream if possible.

Peach Heaven

This is always voted an absolute wow!

> At least one big peach per head (tinned peaches will do)

brandy
1 carton double cream
brown sugar

Peel and slice the peaches into a fireproof dish. Add some brandy – not enough to soak fruit. Coat with a thick layer of stiffly whipped cream. Leave in the fridge for several hours until the cream is pretty hard. Sprinkle with a good layer of brown sugar. Put under a very hot grill until the sugar caramelizes and trickles into the dissolving cream. Eat at once.

SERVES 6.

This recipe is equally good using grapes and whipping up the cream with the brandy, etc.

Peaches in Red Wine

Easy and expensive-looking but can be dirt cheap in the peach season.

6–9 yellow peaches
sugar
$\frac{1}{3}$ bottle of red wine

Pour boiling water over the peaches and leave for a couple of minutes. Skin them, and slice into individual wine goblets. Sprinkle with sugar and then pour the wine over them.

SERVES 6.

Sherry Pears

You can't fail with this.

275 ml ($\frac{1}{2}$ pint) single cream
4 good eating pears
1 tablespoon sherry

    1 heaped tablespoon castor sugar
    sliced almonds *or* walnuts for garnish

Pour the cream into a largish bowl and whip until thick but not stiff. Peel and quarter the pears and very gently stir them into the cream, making sure they are well covered. Divide the pears among four glass dishes. Into the remaining cream, beat the sugar and sherry. Pour it over the pears (use a rubber spatula to get it all up) and decorate with nuts. Chill.

SERVES 4.

Black Treacle Pears

A marvellous recipe for using very hard pears (windfalls will do).

    pears
    black treacle
    brown sugar
    cream
    brandy

Wash the pears and put them in a fireproof dish. (Do not peel or slice.) Pour some black treacle over them and sprinkle with brown sugar. Add a little water. Bake them in a slow oven for about 4 hours. They should look wrinkled and brown – so don't fret. Serve with the cream whipped with brandy.

SERVES as many as you want.

Wine-baked Pears

Make this the night before your dinner party.

    6 pears
    ⅓ bottle white wine

sugar
275 ml (½ pint) double cream

Peel the pears and put in a fireproof dish. Cover with the
wine, sprinkle with a little sugar and bake in a moderate
oven for about 45 minutes. Chill. Serve with whipped
cream.

SERVES 6.

Port-baked Plums

*This recipe is nicer than stewed plums and requires the
same effort.*

  450 g (1 lb) slightly under-ripe plums
  3 tablespoons brown sugar
  2 tablespoons port
  2 tablespoons water
  1 small carton double cream

Wash the plums and split them along the dent. Put all the
ingredients except the cream into an ovenproof dish and
bake in a moderate oven for about 45 minutes or until they
are tender but still whole. Serve hot or cold with cream.

SERVES 3 to 4.

Brandy Prune Fool

*There are so many different varieties of tinned fruits in the
shops so don't be afraid to vary the fruit perhaps.*

  2 medium-size tins prunes
  150 ml (¼ pint) cream
  2 tablespoons brandy
  a few almonds to decorate

Stone the prunes and liquidize with half the juice. Whip

the cream and add to the prunes together with the brandy.
Pour into individual glasses and decorate with a few
almonds. Chill.

SERVES 6.

Raspberry Delight

*If you are talented enough to make a cup of tea with a tea
bag and boiling water you'll be able to manage this no-
trouble pudding.*

> 275 ml (½ pint) double cream
> 2 tablespoons sherry *or* Kirsch
> 2 cartons plain yoghurt
> 450 g (1 lb) raspberries (2 packets frozen)

Whip the cream until stiff but not buttery. Add the liquor,
fold in the yoghurt. Very gently stir in the raspberries –
try not to break them all up – and pour into the bowl or
bowls from which the dessert will be served. Cool in fridge.

SERVES 6 to 8.

Strawberries, loganberries, gooseberries and others would
be just as nice, though cook them or sweeten them as needs
must.

Raspberry Gâteau

*You can just as easily use strawberries or any other fruit in
season varying the liqueur to suit what you use. This is
simple to prepare and is much better for having been done
well in advance.*

> 125 g (4 oz) butter
> 125 g (4 oz) castor sugar
> 125 g (4 oz) ground almonds
> 4 tablespoons double cream

2 packets boudoir biscuits *or* sponge fingers
Kirsch
225 g (8 oz) raspberries

Line a 12½-cm (5-inch) or 15-cm (6-inch) cake tin with a loose base with greaseproof paper.

Beat the butter and sugar until creamy, add the ground almonds and beat a little longer. Stir in the cream.

Cover the base of the tin with the sponge fingers. Sprinkle with Kirsch. Spread half the cream mixture on the fingers. Put the raspberries on top of cream and sprinkle them with sugar (omit this sugar if you've not such a sweet tooth). Cover with the rest of the cream and press more sponge fingers gently on top. Sprinkle with Kirsch.

Leave for at least 24 hours and then push gently out of the tin. Decorate with whipped cream and raspberries.

SERVES 6.

Raspberry and Kirsch Mousse

This I love. Strawberries can be used instead of raspberries if there's a glut.

2 large punnets raspberries
a little castor sugar to taste
2 tablespoons Kirsch
1 large carton double cream
2 egg whites
pinch salt

Put the raspberries into your liquidizer and purée them. Add a very little sugar and the Kirsch. Put into a jug and keep covered. Whisk the cream until thick and the egg whites until stiff (with the pinch of salt). Fold them together and leave in the fridge until they begin to set. Then whisk them again and fold in the purée.

Pour into a serving dish and leave in the fridge until required.

SERVES 4 to 6.

Rhubarb Fool

More unusual than strawberry etc. and can be made at a time of year when cold puddings are not quite so expected.

    900 g (2 lb) rhubarb
    75 g (3 oz) butter
    350 g (12 oz) sugar
    1 tablespoon lemon juice
    550 ml (1 pint) double cream
    1 tablespoon brandy *or* orange liqueur

Wash the rhubarb and cut it up. Melt the butter, add the sugar, fruit and lemon juice and bring to the boil. Keep stirring until the fruit is soft but not slushy. Allow to cool.

Liquidize in a blender, then chill until just before you eat. Whip the cream, add the liqueur, fold into the fruit mixture. If this is too sour (and deliberately this is not very sweet) add a little more sugar.

SERVES 8.

Strawberries and Cream

This is a conventional idea prepared in an unconventional way.

    1½ litres (3 pints) strawberries
    granulated sugar
    2 tablespoons cherry brandy
    275 ml (½ pint) double cream
    275 ml (½ pint) sour cream
    pistachio nuts to decorate

Hull the strawberries and wash if necessary – I always avoid the latter if possible as they go so mushy. Put them in a bowl and sprinkle with granulated sugar. Add the liqueur and chill them for several hours.

Just before serving, whisk the cream until it just begins to thicken and blend it with the sour cream (do not whip it). Pour the cream over the strawberries and sprinkle with chopped nuts.

SERVES 6 to 8.

Strawberry and Orange Dessert

>   3 oranges
>   450 g (1 lb) strawberries
>   225 g (8 oz) castor sugar
>   150 ml (¼ pint) water
>   2 tablespoons lemon juice (Jif)
>   2 tablespoons of Grand Marnier *or* Cointreau

Cut a slice off the top and bottom of the oranges and then place them on a flat board and cut downwards with a knife to remove the peel and the pith. Slice the oranges thinly, remove all pips, and place in a serving dish. Hull the strawberries and arrange over the oranges. Melt the sugar in the water over a low heat, stirring constantly. Remove from heat and add the lemon juice and the liqueur. Allow to cool and then pour over the fruit and chill.

SERVES 6.

Strawberry Cream

A nice dinner-party sweet to serve when strawberries alone are no longer a treat.

>   3 punnets strawberries
>   50 g (2 oz) sugar
>   1 tablespoon Kirsch
>   1 tablespoon Cointreau
>   1 tablespoon light rum
>   275 ml (½ pint) double cream
>   1 975 g (34 oz) block vanilla ice cream

Wipe and hull the strawberries. In the serving bowl crush

them slightly and add the sugar and the three liqueurs. Whip the cream and mix together with the ice cream. Pour the cream over the strawberries and leave to chill for about 30 minutes.

SERVES a good 8.

Strawberry Jelly

This is nearly as nice as wild strawberries sprinkled with wine but sadly wild strawberries don't happen very often.

> 450 g (1 lb) strawberries
> juice of $\frac{1}{2}$ lemon
> a little sugar
> $\frac{1}{2}$ bottle sweet white wine
> 14 g ($\frac{1}{2}$ oz) gelatine

Halve the strawberries and arrange them in a suitable bowl. Sprinkle with the lemon juice and the sugar. Heat the wine, being careful not to boil it, and add the gelatine which has already been dissolved in a little hot water. Stir occasionally until the gelatine is dissolved and the wine is cool. Pour over the strawberries and leave to set. This is better served without cream.

SERVES 4 to 6.

Bavarian Strawberry Flan

Easy and can be made a day in advance.

> 675 g (1 lb 8 oz) strawberries (strained tinned ones can also be used)
> 3 tablespoons castor sugar
> 1 envelope (14 g ($\frac{1}{2}$ oz)) gelatine
> 4 tablespoons cold water
> 1 tablespoon Grand Marnier
> 225 ml (8 oz) double cream
> 1 large sponge flan case

Hull the strawberries and, keeping aside a few for decoration, mash the rest to give 425 ml ($\frac{3}{4}$ pint) of pulp. Stir in sugar to taste. Dissolve the gelatine in a little water; stir into the strawberry mixture and add the Grand Marnier. Put this into the fridge until it begins to thicken slightly.

Meanwhile whisk the cream with 1 or 2 teaspoons castor sugar and a pinch of salt until thick but not buttery. Add the strawberry mixture and fill the flan with it. Chill. Decorate with whole strawberries and fresh sprigs of mint.

SERVES 6 to 8.

Elizabethan Flan

And it's delicious.

2 large thin-skinned oranges
2 tablespoons honey
150 ml ($\frac{1}{4}$ pint) water
225 g (8 oz) rich short-crust pastry
150 ml ($\frac{1}{4}$ pint) double cream
1 tablespoon brandy
50 g (2 oz) granulated sugar

Wash the oranges and cut into thin rings, the peel should be kept on. Soak overnight in honey and water. Next day place the oranges and liquid in a pan and simmer for 25–30 minutes. Drain and cool, keeping the liquid.

Put a 20-cm (8-inch) flan dish on a baking sheet and line with the pastry. Bake 'blind', i.e. cover with grease-proof paper and fill with rice or beans, etc. to weigh it down, in a moderately hot oven for 15 minutes. Remove the paper and filling and cook for a further 10 minutes until pale gold. Cool.

Whip the cream until just stiff, add the brandy and spread over bottom of the flan case. Overlap the orange slices on top. Add the sugar to 150 ml ($\frac{1}{4}$ pint) of the honey liquid and heat gently until the sugar has dissolved. Bring to the boil and cook until syrup consistency, 3–5 minutes. Pour this gently over the oranges and cream.

SERVES 4 to 6.

Rum and Chocolate Flan

This benefits by being made in advance so that the ice cream can melt a little, which makes it easier to spread.

> 125 g (4 oz) dark chocolate
> 50 g (2 oz) cornflakes
> 4 McVitie's trifle sponges
> 4 tablespoons rum
> 1 484 g (17 oz) block chocolate-ripple ice cream

Melt three-quarters of the chocolate in a non-stick pan and gently stir in the cornflakes until they are evenly coated with chocolate. Spread a 15-cm (6-inch) soufflé dish with the mixture and chill. Crumble the trifle sponges and mix them with the rum. Spread on top of the cornflakes. Put the chocolate ice cream on top of this and decorate with the rest of the chocolate, grated. Chill until wanted.

SERVES 6.

Auld Alliance Cream

This is delicious, very easy (except that you have to think about it two days in advance) and provided there is a whisky drinker in the house, very cheap.

> 225 g (8 oz) prunes
> 275 ml ($\frac{1}{2}$ pint) water
> 1 glass whisky
> grated rind and juice of $\frac{1}{2}$ lemon
> $\frac{1}{4}$ teaspoon ground ginger
> 25 g (1 oz) sugar
> 275 ml ($\frac{1}{2}$ pint) hot water
> 1 lemon jelly
> $2\frac{1}{2}$-cm (1-inch) cinnamon stick
> 4 cloves
> whipped cream and nuts to decorate

Wash the prunes and soak them in half a pint of water and the whisky for about 48 hours. Don't cook them. Then remove the stones and liquidize until smooth. Stir in the lemon rind and juice, ginger and sugar. Pour half a pint of hot water over the jelly, cinnamon and cloves. Stir until dissolved, if necessary reheat a little. Allow to cool. Strain the liquid into the prune mixture and leave until it starts to set. Stir well. Pour into individual glasses or one large bowl. Decorate with cream and nuts.

SERVES 6.

Biskotten Torte

This is a rich pudding which takes some time to prepare but is very easy. It is much better made a couple of days before you need it, but do allow at least 24 hours or the full taste doesn't emerge.

175 g (6 oz) butter
175 g (6 oz) castor sugar
1 egg
125 g (4 oz) walnuts and a few more for decoration
2 coffee spoons instant coffee
25 g (1 oz) butter
25 g (1 oz) flour
150 ml ($\frac{1}{4}$ pint) milk
4 tablespoons brandy *or* Tia Maria
2 packets boudoir biscuits
teacupful of milk
275 ml ($\frac{1}{2}$ pint) double cream for decoration

Beat the butter and sugar vigorously. When pale add the egg and continue beating until creamy. Mince the walnuts and add with the coffee powder.

Melt 25 g (1 oz) butter, add the flour and cook gently for 1 minute. Add the milk all at once and cook for 5 minutes stirring continuously. Leave to cool. Then add a spoonful at a time to the walnut mixture.

Line a 15-cm (6-inch) cake tin with greaseproof paper. Add the liqueur to the milk. Dip the sponge fingers very lightly in the liqueur mixture. (Be careful not to saturate the fingers or they become soggy and unpalatable.) Line the bottom and sides of the tin with them. Then fill the tin with a layer of walnut cream, dipped fingers, walnut cream and end with dipped fingers. Cover with grease-proof paper and put in the fridge.

Turn out gently (it can collapse). Whip the double cream and cover the pudding with it. Decorate with walnuts if desired (ground if you have the time).

SERVES 8 to 10.

Calvados Glory

This concoction was invented on the spur of the moment when a load of uninvited guests turned up to be fed. It was immediately successful and required very little effort. Try it.

4 trifle sponges
1 tablespoon Calvados
225 g (8 oz) apple jelly
150 ml (¼ pint) double cream
almonds or ratafias to garnish (optional)

Slice the sponges in half and use them to line a shallow serving dish. Sprinkle with Calvados. Warm the jelly to the point where it is no longer solid. There is no need to melt it entirely. Spread this over the sponges as evenly as possible. Put the mixture in the fridge to cool off. Beat the cream. You can thin it down with a little single cream as well. Spread this over your dessert, decorate with nuts if you care to and serve when you will.

SERVES 4 to 6.

Cheeze Freeze

Child's play and rich.

    1 small carton double cream
    1 small carton cottage cheese
    1 small jar black cherry jam
    1–2 tablespoons Kirsch

Whip the cream until stiff and stir into the cheese. Spoon it into individual ramekins and freeze. Just before serving heat the jam with the Kirsch. Either pour the sauce into each ramekin or pass it separately.

SERVES 4 to 6 depending on the ramekins.

This can also be made with marmalade and whisky.

Rich Glorious Chocolate Mousse

Never fails, always pleases.

    175 g (6 oz) good dark chocolate
    1 tablespoon water
    5 eggs
    2 tablespoons brandy
    salt

In a double pan melt the broken-up chocolate with the water. Cook gently, stirring vigorously until the chocolate is smooth. Allow to cool to body temperature. Separate the eggs and beat in the yolks one by one. Stir in the liqueur. Whisk the egg whites with a pinch of salt. When stiff, fold them into the mousse. Either pour into a glass serving dish or distribute between individual dishes.

    This SERVES 6, but if you arrange a layer of liqueur-soaked boudoir biscuits at the bottom of your serving dish, it will easily feed 8.

Chocolate Brandy Trifle (1)

A good rich pudding which should be served very cold.

        175 g (6 oz) plain chocolate
        1 teacup milk
        1 packet Lyons sponge cakes *or* McVitie's trifle
            sponges
        3 tablespoons brandy
        50 g (2 oz) ratafias *or* chopped macaroons
        275 ml (½ pint) double cream

Grate 125 g (4 oz) of the chocolate. Melt the remaining chocolate in the milk over a low heat. Cool. Line a large shallow dish with the sponge cakes cut in half – inside uppermost. Mix the brandy into the chocolate and pour the lot over the cakes. Sprinkle with ratafias or macaroons. Whip the cream and fold in most of the grated chocolate. Pile this into the bowl and decorate with the remaining chocolate.

SERVES 6 to 8.

Chocolate Brandy Trifle (2)

A variation on the previous recipe.

        2 packets boudoir biscuits
        3 tablespoons sherry
        3 tablespoons brandy
        175 g (6 oz) plain chocolate
        a little water
        275 ml (½ pint) double cream

Dip the boudoir biscuits in the sherry and brandy and arrange in rows across a serving bowl. Melt most of the chocolate in water and pour some of it over the biscuits. Arrange another row of dipped biscuits at right angles to the first. Cover with chocolate. Continue until supplies run out. (The number of layers depends on the size and shape of the bowl.) Whip the cream and pile on top of the layers.

Grate the remaining chocolate and sprinkle over the cream.

SERVES 6 to 8.

Chocolate Sludge

A descriptive but inelegant title which shouldn't put you off this rich dessert. But don't serve it after too heavy courses – it won't be so enjoyable.

6 tablespoons Kirsch
200 g (7 oz) crumbled petit beurre biscuits
225 g (8 oz) chocolate chips *or* chocolate Meunier
4 tablespoons water
200 g (7 oz) butter
4 separated eggs
200 g (7 oz) icing sugar
125 g (4 oz) peeled grapes (*or* drained tinned grapes)
1 large carton cream
icing sugar to decorate

Sprinkle the Kirsch over the crushed biscuits and leave to soak. Very gently dissolve the chocolate in the water. Stir until smooth and then take off the heat. Gradually add the butter, stir until the chocolate absorbs it all. Add the egg yolks and stir until smooth, then repeat with the sugar. Beat the egg whites until stiff and then add them. Then stir in the biscuit mixture and the grapes. Finally add the cream.

Oil a loose-bottomed cake tin and then line it with a circle of oiled greaseproof paper. Pour in the mixture and chill.

Immediately before serving, turn out and dredge with icing sugar.

This is, *par excellence*, a dessert that can be made well in advance.

SERVES 8.

Coffee Marshmallow with Brandy Cream

A rather interesting pudding which amuses people who never guess what makes it gell.

   40 marshmallows
   275 ml (½ pint) very strong instant black coffee
   275 ml (½ pint) double cream
   1 tablespoon brandy
   flaked almonds *or* walnuts for decoration

Cut the marshmallows up into four (marginally sticky job, easiest when done with kitchen scissors). Put them in a large bowl with the boiling coffee. Whisk until they dissolve and the mixture froths. Turn into a large serving bowl or individual glasses. Allow to cool.

Whip the cream until fairly stiff. Add the brandy. Spread over the pudding and decorate with almonds (or walnuts, as you will).

SERVES 6 to 8.

Gin Torte

Gin is not widely used in cooking but having tasted this you'll long to find more excuses for flavouring with gin.

   150 g (5 oz) castor sugar
   3 eggs
   125 g (4 oz) butter
   100 g (3½ oz) ground almonds
   50 g (2 oz) self-raising flour
   icing:
   125 (4 oz) icing sugar
   1 generous tablespoon gin

Beat the sugar and eggs until thick and fluffy. Soften the butter. Work it into the mixture together with the almonds and flour. Mix thoroughly.

Bake in a well-buttered tin for 15 minutes until firm (Gas 7 or 220°C (425°F)). Cool.

Just before serving, mix the icing sugar with the gin and spread on top of the cake. If you do this too far in advance, you will sadly lose the aroma of the liquor.

SERVES 4 to 6.

Port Jelly

So many people have never tasted anything but commercial jellies, they'll be delighted by the soft flavour and texture of this one.

> 125 g (4 oz) sugar
> 275 ml ($\frac{1}{2}$ pint) water
> 1 tablespoon redcurrant *or* apple jelly
> $2\frac{1}{2}$ cm (1 inch) or so of cinnamon stick
> 3 cloves
> 1 lemon
> 14 g ($\frac{1}{2}$ oz) gelatine
> 275 ml ($\frac{1}{2}$ pint) port

In a scrupulously clean pan gently heat the sugar, water, jelly, cinnamon, cloves and juice and finely pared rind of the lemon. Dissolve the gelatine in a very little water and stir that in. Then continue simmering for a few minutes longer. Stir in the port. Strain until clear through muslin and allow to cool a little. Then rinse the jelly mould in cold water and pour the jelly in. Leave to set. Turn out just before serving.

SERVES 4.

Ginger Wine Jellies

This recipe is not for children, perhaps, but you can always try it out on them.

> 275 ml ($\frac{1}{2}$ pint) less 1 tablespoon cold water
> 14 g ($\frac{1}{2}$ oz) gelatine

rind and juice of 1 lemon
3 tablespoons sugar
275 ml ($\frac{1}{2}$ pint) ginger wine
whipped cream
boudoir biscuits

Put the water into a saucepan, add the gelatine and leave
for a few minutes. Add the thinly pared lemon rind and
heat slowly, stirring all the time, until all the gelatine has
dissolved. Add the sugar and dissolve. Remove from heat
and leave to stand for about 10 minutes. Add the ginger
wine and lemon juice and leave to cool. Strain through
muslin into individual glasses. Chill. Decorate with a layer
of cream and serve with boudoir biscuits.

SERVES 4

This is equally good made with port wine, and adding a $1\frac{1}{4}$-
cm ($\frac{1}{2}$-inch) piece of cinnamon to infuse with the lemon
rind and water.

Liqueur Soufflé

*Very simple and it can all be prepared in advance bar beat-
ing the egg whites.*

sponge cake
liqueur
4 eggs
$3\frac{1}{2}$ tablespoons sugar
1 tablespoon liqueur

Line a soufflé dish with a thin layer of sponge cake and
sprinkle it liberally with liqueur. Separate the eggs. Beat
the yolks until they pale. Add the sugar and keep beating;
when they are creamy add the liqueur.

Beat the egg whites until stiff. Fold the two mixtures
together and pour into a soufflé dish. Bake in a hot oven for
10 minutes.

(If you use orange liqueurs, add the grated rind of one orange.)

SERVES 4.

Frosted Liqueur Mousse

    1 large egg white
    150 ml (¼ pint) double cream
    2 level tablespoons icing sugar
    2 tablespoons apricot brandy, Chartreuse, Grand
        Marnier, brandy *or* rum
    a few chopped toasted nuts

Whisk the egg white until stiff. In another bowl whisk the cream until it is just beginning to thicken, add the sifted icing sugar and continue whipping until the cream is thick but not too stiff. Fold in the egg white and the liqueur. Spoon into individual ramekin dishes, sprinkle with nuts and freeze until firm.

SERVES 4.

Norwegian Cream

This is a good pudding to serve after a hot curry as it is very light.

    425 ml (¾ pint) milk
    1½ dessertspoons sugar
    3 eggs
    vanilla essence
    3 tablespoons apricot jam
    2 tablespoons apricot brandy
    3 tablespoons cream
    chocolate

Boil the milk with the sugar. Keep back 1 egg white and put the other eggs and whites in a separate basin. Beat slightly with vanilla essence. Pour over the milk when hot but not boiling. Put jam and brandy in the bottom of a dish. Pour in the strained custard. Stand in water and bake in a moderate oven covered with foil until set. Remove from the oven. When cold beat the remaining egg white, fold into the cream. Beat the cream and cover the pudding. Sprinkle with grated chocolate.

SERVES 4.

Ginger Brandy

This pudding is even more scrummy if allowed to chill for about 48 hours.

425 ml (¾ pint) double cream
2 packets gingernut biscuits
1 large mug strong black coffee doused with brandy

Whip the cream until stiff. Dip the biscuits in the coffee mixture one by one and put alternate layers of biscuits and cream until all ingredients are used, making sure to leave enough cream aside to decorate the top just before serving (so that it doesn't go brown). Cover the pudding, preferably with a weighted plate and leave to chill overnight or preferably much longer. Decorate with cream before serving.

SERVES 8.

Puff Pastry Gâteau

This looks most professional and is so easy and quick to make.

1 packet frozen puff pastry
a small carton double cream
1 tablespoon fruit liqueur *or* sherry
fresh *or* tinned fruit
icing sugar for decoration

Roll the pastry until extremely thin – should be a rectangular shape. Bake in a moderate oven for about 20 minutes or until it has risen and is golden on the outside and cooked inside. Remove from the oven and slit with a knife lengthways in half. If this should reveal some uncooked pastry on the inside, either remove it, or put the two halves back into the oven at a low heat to dry out. Whip the cream together with liquor and add the fruit. When the pastry is fairly cool, fill the case with the fruit mixture, put the lid on top and sprinkle with sieved icing sugar.

SERVES 4.

Crêpes Suzette

A world favourite spectacular, easily made in this way.

> 175 g (6 oz) flour
> 3 eggs
> 1½ tablespoons castor sugar
> 425 ml (¾ pint) milk
> 1½ tablespoons oil
> 1½ tablespoons brandy
> 150 g (5 oz) butter
> 150 g (5 oz) castor sugar
> finely grated rind of 1 *or* 2 oranges
> 3 tablespoons orange liqueur
> plus 4 *or* 5 more tablespoons brandy *or* liqueur to flame

Sift the flour into a large bowl and break the eggs into the middle of it. Stir them until the mixture is smooth then add the sugar and the milk. You are supposed to leave the mixture to stand for a couple of hours but I never do and it doesn't seem to matter. Just before cooking stir in the oil and brandy and mix well. Melt a little butter in a small pan and fry as many very thin pancakes as you can get out of the mixture.

Meanwhile, with a fork, mash the butter and sugar and

when well mixed add the orange rind and liqueur.

As each pancake is made, spread it with a little of the butter mixture. Roll the pancakes up and arrange in an ovenproof dish. When all are made, sprinkle with a little sugar and try to keep fairly warm. Put in a hot oven for less than 10 minutes and at the table pour hot brandy or liqueur over them, ignite and consume at once. Delicious.

SERVES 6.

Pancakes filled with Fruit

This is delicious, filling and impressive-looking. Making the pancakes is far more boring than making the filling.

> 8 small thin pancakes
> 25 g (1 oz) butter
> a very little lemon juice
> 2 apples
> 2 tablespoons apricot jam
> ½ small carton double cream
> 2 tablespoons Calvados
> a few macaroons *or* ratafias

Having made the pancakes, stack them on a Pyrex dish one on top of another, separated by greaseproof paper. Put the dish on a pan of hot water and keep it hot. A piece of foil loosely over the lot ensures that they stay warm without getting soggy.

Melt the butter with the lemon juice. Peel, core and chop the apples, add to the butter and cook them until soft. Then stir in the jam. Whip the cream, stir in the Calvados and add to the apple mixture. This is the stuffing. Fill the pancakes, roll them up and arrange in a fireproof dish. Sprinkle with crushed macaroons or ratafias and a little sugar and leave under a hot grill until caramelly on top (this takes no time at all). Eat at once.

SERVES 4.

Rum Omelette

When I was a very little girl living in Malta we used to lunch out at least two Sundays a month at the Melitta Hotel. I always had rum omelettes, which were probably the first alcoholic desserts I came across. This is how they were made – I remember finding out at the time.

4 eggs
1 tablespoon sugar
a pinch of salt
2 tablespoons dark jam, cherry, strawberry *or* plum
castor sugar for garnish
3 tablespoons rum

Separate the eggs. Stir the yolks with the sugar, beat the whites with salt until stiff and fold into the yolk mixture. Cook the omelette, fill with the warmed jam, fold over, slide on to a fireproof dish and sprinkle with sugar. Then place it under a hot grill for a second or two. Meanwhile warm the rum, pour it over the omelette, set it alight and eat at once. Heaven.

SERVES 2.

Other schools of thought omit the jam, others don't separate the eggs or beat the egg whites. Still others fill their omelette with warmed fruit rather than jam. Many people like more sugar, still others prefer their omelettes flamed with Pernod or scented spirits. All are good, but I have my loyalties.

Hot Ginger Soufflé

40 g (1½ oz) butter
40 g (1½ oz) flour
275 ml (½ pint) milk
75 g (3 oz) sugar
1 tablespoon brandy
a good pinch powdered ginger

50 g (2 oz) chopped, preserved ginger
4 eggs
whipped cream
ginger syrup

Make a thick white sauce with the butter, flour and milk and cook for a couple of minutes. Add the sugar, brandy and ginger. Separate the egg yolks, and beat into the mixture one at a time. Whisk the egg whites until stiff and then fold them into the mixture. Pour it into a prepared 17½-cm (7-inch) soufflé dish. Bake in a moderate oven for about 45 minutes or until well risen and firm on top. Serve at once with whipped cream and ginger syrup.

SERVES a good 4.

Chocolate Rum Soufflé

Very rich, very delicious.

550 ml (1 pint) milk
6 medium eggs
50 g (2 oz) self-raising flour
225 g (8 oz) castor sugar
135 g (4½ oz) dark chocolate
2 tablespoons rum
14 g (½ oz) powdered gelatine (*or* 1 packet)
4 tablespoons water
275 ml (½ pint) double cream
chocolate for decoration

Heat the milk until almost boiling (do not boil). Separate the eggs and set aside the whites. In the top of a double saucepan beat together the egg yolks, flour and sugar. Then add the milk and stir until the mixture thickens. Grate the chocolate and add to the mixture. Remove from the heat and stir until the chocolate has melted. Beat vigorously and add the rum. Pour into a large bowl. Completely dissolve the gelatine in the boiling water and beat into the mixture. Whip the cream, and add to the mixture. Whisk the egg whites until stiff and fold in. Place the bowl in a larger bowl of ice and whip the whole mixture until it begins to wrinkle. Sellotape a piece of foil around a soufflé dish with three inches jutting over the top, pour the soufflé into the dish and leave to set in a cool place. Decorate with chocolate leaves made by washing a few rose leaves, melting 125 g (4 oz) of dark chocolate in a non-stick pan and coating one side of the leaves by dragging them over the chocolate. Allow them to cool and then peel off the leaves.

SERVES 6 to 8.

Sherry Cream

Should anyone give you some sweet sherry and should you not be too keen on sweet sherry you can use it to make up this recipe of Helen Burke's which is both very good and very easy – much nicer than drinking sweet sherry.

7 g (¼ oz) gelatine
3 tablespoons water
4 tablespoons sweet sherry
2 eggs
50 g (2 oz) castor sugar
salt
150 ml (¼ pint) double cream

Soak the gelatine in the water, then dissolve it over a low heat. Add the sherry.

Separate the eggs. Beat the yolks and sugar until they are fluffy and then stir in the gelatine mixture. Add a tiny pinch of salt to the whites and beat them till stiff. Fold them into the mixture. Then beat the cream (don't bother washing the whisk) until it is thicker but not stiff. Fold that in too. Turn into serving dish and chill.

SERVES 4.

If the pudding is made a day in advance take it out of the fridge well in advance of the meal or it will be too stiff.

Whisky Cream

Where this recipe originated from I don't know, but since a magazine published it about a year ago I seem to have eaten it at most people's homes.

    7 g (¼ oz) gelatine
    75 ml (⅛ pint) cold water
    150 ml (¼ pint) double cream
    150 ml (¼ pint) single cream
    1 good tablespoon clear honey
    2 tablespoons whisky

Dissolve the gelatine in the water. Whip the double cream until fairly thick, then add the single cream and keep whipping until both thicken. Gently whip the honey and the whisky. Fold in dissolved gelatine, keep folding until the mixture starts to set. You have to persevere or it will separate a bit. Pour into individual serving dishes (it looks pretty in glass) and chill.

SERVES 4.

Whisky and Oatmeal Syllabub

    25 g (1 oz) medium oatmeal
    275 ml (½ pint) double cream
    125 ml (4 oz) honey
    5 tablespoons whisky
    1 teaspoon Jif lemon juice

Sprinkle the oatmeal on a flat, fireproof dish and toast under the grill until golden, shaking occasionally so that it does not burn. Whip the cream until stiff. Mix together the honey, whisky and lemon juice, add to the cream and whip until very stiff. Fold in 1 tablespoon oatmeal. Pile the mixture into glasses and chill. Sprinkle with the remaining oatmeal before serving.

SERVES 6.

Hot Zabaglione

This is a knack – if you've got it you serve a memorable pudding, if not the dog has boozy scrambled eggs for supper.

> 6 egg yolks
> 50 g (2 oz) castor sugar
> 5 tablespoons Marsala
> ratafia biscuits *or* boudoir fingers

Put the first three ingredients in a double saucepan, making quite sure that the top half doesn't touch the water. Whisk over a low heat until the mixture lightens in colour and thickens in texture. Pour immediately into individual glasses and serve with the biscuits. It must be eaten at once.

SERVES 6.

Stilton with Port

Should you have bought a whole Stilton and be left with all the crumbling bits, this is so good you might almost be tempted to go out and buy Stilton to make it from scratch. It is currently very smart to sneer at it, but try it for your-self – I like it.

> Stilton
> port

Mash however much Stilton you have with a fork. Then add the port little by little and mash it in. Get the cheese to take as much liquor as possible. Pack it into a serving dish and eat with biscuits.

Cream Cheese with Wine

This is a slightly more mundane alternative to the Stilton with Port but still good.

450 g (1 lb) cream cheese
50 g (2 oz) castor sugar
1 large glass white wine
juice of a lemon

Mash the cheese. Then gradually work in the sugar, wine
and lemon juice. This is also served with biscuits.

SERVES 4.

Black Forest Ice Cream

This German recipe is simple and good.

1 tin black cherries
1 tablespoon Kirsch
1 484 g (17 oz) block Cornish ice cream
1 small carton double cream
a few almonds for decoration

Strain the juice from the cherries into a pan with the Kirsch.
Warm it. Meanwhile divide the ice cream into four and
put each piece into the bottom of a sundae glass. Divide
the cherries among the glasses. Whip the cream until thick.
Spoon that over the ice cream and cherries, by which time
the juice ought to be just the right temperature (not so hot
as to melt everything at once). Pour that over the top,
sprinkle with almonds and serve at once.

SERVES 4.

Peppermint Chocolate Ice

*This is equally good made with either cream or ice cream
and couldn't be easier.*

1 975 g (34 oz) block Cornish ice cream *or* 550 ml (1
pint) whipped cream
50 g (2 oz) grated Bournville chocolate
3–4 tablespoons Crème de Menthe

Allow the ice cream to thaw slightly. Mix all the ingredients together and decorate with a little grated chocolate. Freeze.

SERVES 6.

Rum and Raisin Ice Cream

This has to be prepared at least 3 hours in advance, but apart from that slight complication takes longer to wash up than make.

> 1 975 g (34 oz) block Cornish ice cream
> 2 tablespoons rum
> 125 g (4 oz) sultanas

Allow the ice cream to thaw slightly. Stir in the other ingredients. Pour into a serving dish. Freeze. (If you have got time, the raisins are delicious soaked in the rum beforehand.)

SERVES 6.

Zabaglione Ice Cream

These two Helen Burke recipes make delicious ice cream but as they are made from frozen cream, they must be taken out of the freezer at least 15 minutes before serving – or they will not taste so good.

> 3 large egg yolks
> 3 heaped teaspoons sugar
> 4 tablespoons Marsala
> 150 ml ($\frac{1}{4}$ pint) double cream
> flaked toasted almonds to decorate

Beat the egg yolks and sugar until creamy. Add the Marsala and beat over hot water (but not touching or it will scramble) until fairly stiff. Take off the heat and continue beating until cold. Whip the cream and fold into the mixture. Pour into a suitable vessel and freeze.

SERVES 4.

A Kind of Cassata

    2 tablespoons currants
    2 tablespoons sultanas
    1 tablespoon chopped orange peel
    1 tablespoon chopped glacé cherries
    1 tablespoon flaked almonds
    1 tablespoon brandy
    1 tablespoon orange juice
    275 ml ($\frac{1}{2}$ pint) double cream
    1 tablespoon icing sugar

Soak the fruit and nuts in the brandy and orange juice in a screw-top jar overnight. Shake it every now and then. Whip the cream and sugar until fairly stiff. Fold in the fruit and mix well. Pour it into a pretty dish and freeze.

SERVES 4.

INDEX